Sleep Training for Babies:

The Step-By-Step Plan for Helping Your Newborn Baby Sleep Better

By:
Ava Burke

Copyright © 2020 by Ava Burke

ALL RIGHTS RESERVED

No part of this book may be reproduced, stored in a retrieval system, or transmitted in any form or by any means, electronic, mechanical, photocopying, recording, scanning, or otherwise, without the prior written permission of the publisher.

Limit of Liability/Disclaimer of Warranty: the publisher and the author make no representations or warranties with respect to the accuracy or completeness of the contents of this work and specifically disclaim all warranties, including without limitation warranties of fitness for a particular purpose. No warranty may be created or extended by sales or promotional materials. The advice and strategies contained herein may not be suitable for every situation. This work is sold with the understanding that the publisher is not engaged in rendering medical, legal or other professional advice or services. If professional assistance is required, the services of a competent professional person should be sought. Neither the publisher nor the author shall be liable for damages arising herefrom. The fact that an individual, organization or website is referred to in this work as a citation and/or potential source of further information does not mean that the author or the publisher endorses the information the individuals, organization or website may provide or recommendations they/it may make. Further, readers should be aware that websites listed on this work may have changed or disappeared between when this work was written and when it is read.

ISBN: 978-1-951791-61-2

10-POINT CHECKLIST YOUR BABY IS READY FOR SLEEP TRAINING

Visit:

Avaburke.org/sleep

Contents

Introduction 5

Chapter 1. Understanding the Importance of Healthy Sleep 9

Chapter 2. The Science behind Sleep Training 16

Chapter 3. Preparing to Sleep Train your Baby 22

Chapter 4. Creating a Sleep Friendly Environment 33

Chapter 5. Sleep Safety, Sleep Props and Swaddling 41

Chapter 6. Establish a Consistent Routine 48

Chapter 7. Self- Soothing: Letting your baby put themselves to sleep 54

Chapter 8. Week 1 of Sleep Training 59

Chapter 9. Conquering Naps 72

Chapter 10. Baby let's get some sleep! 79

Introduction

Congratulations on the new addition to your family and welcome to parenthood. You've spent the last nine months preparing, nesting, and enjoying some much-needed quality time with your partner before the arrival of your newest family member. Excitement surrounds you and you probably can't wait to see your baby grow and develop for many years to come. But now you find yourself on a foreign planet without a tour guide or a road map. You are now embarking on one of the biggest changes in your life. You are becoming a parent. You will officially be fully responsible for a tiny human being. These feelings are exciting, scary, and overwhelming all at once. As a new parent, we are now realizing that our baby needs our attention close to twenty-four hours a day. From the first moment of a child's life, and likely even before the baby arrives, parents are bombarded with ideas and suggestions on parenting styles, programs to follow, and opinions from our friends and family around us. This can make for an incredibly confusing time. A time when things don't make sense and time feels as though it's speeding up and slowing down at the same time. We might even end up with expectations on what to expect with this new baby from those around us. People will want to share their experiences, tell you what you "should" do, and they might even scare you by telling you their parenting horror stories. While it's important to have conversations with friends and family who have children, and even those who don't, we must understand that every child is different and will behave, grow and develop in different ways. When we assume the experience of others will be our own, we often develop unrealistic expectations that can be both good and bad. These thoughts can unfortunately impact the way we parent and might interfere with decisions that we need to make for our children. It's easy to want to listen to those around us and of course, looking to your support system for guidance is always helpful, but take everything with a grain of salt. Your experience with your baby will be your own, unique experience, unlike that of your parents, grandparents, friends, or anyone on social media. Whether this is your first baby, second, or even third, there's simply no way to fully prepare for life with a newborn. Every baby is different, they each have different sleep and eating habits and they are unique in their way. If this isn't your first experience as a parent, you might be expecting your second child to behave like your first, and to be honest, that most likely will not be the case. If your first baby was an excellent sleeper, your next baby might not be. Either way, you can only prepare and plan to a certain degree before simply living in the moment and adjusting to your new life right alongside your newborn.

Remaining flexible and resilient as a parent while building this new relationship with your child. Flexibility is critical for any new relationship, including the relationship you are building with your baby. They, like you, will grow and change over time, develop new habits, and become more engaged in the newfound exciting world around them. One of your jobs, as their parent, is to ensure your child has developed the skills needed to sleep well as a newborn, a toddler, and beyond. Laying the foundation now will ensure your child will be able to self-soothe, become more independent, and identify ways on their own to comfort themselves. While this can be challenging for parents because we feel that we need to do everything in our power to help our babies and children, by providing them with a toolkit to be self-sufficient with good sleep habits, you are setting your child up for success now and long into the future. Developing healthy sleep habits will follow your child through life and you will be happy that you took the right steps to ensure they successfully were able to put themselves to sleep. You will never look back and say to yourself, I wish I wouldn't have sleep trained my baby.

Keep in mind, working with your baby to ensure better sleep will also ensure you and your family sleep better. If your baby is constantly waking up throughout the night, the chances of the caretaker being the only one woken up from these cries are slim. The entire family is likely struggling to sleep around the baby crying and this might even impact the amount of sleep your other children or those living in your household are getting each night. To control the situation and encourage good sleep habits for all those involved, you must first begin with sleep training your baby. This will lead to sleep success for not only your child but for the entire family. Lack of sleep can cause marital problems, arguments between children and parents and it might even impact your neighbors and those who live close to you. Be mindful of those who might be impacted by your child's lack of sleep and try to ensure a proper plan is implemented that is suitable and impactful for all who are involved and would benefit from the outcomes of sleep training your baby. Once you evaluate the situation, you might even find that there are quite a few more people impacted than you even thought.

The more work you can do now to sleep train your baby, the more sleep you will get tomorrow. Remember, this isn't a sprint or a race. This isn't a test to see how quickly you can get your child sleeping through the night. This is a time to develop a clear and consistent routine for you, your baby, and the entire family. If you put in the time and effort and focus on the end goal, you will achieve success. Babies, like adults, take time to truly develop good habits and follow routines. It is not something that happens overnight or with the push of a button. Ensuring that a routine will remain in place calls for consistency. There will be an immense amount of work that goes into the sleep training process and if you're able to focus on the long-term effects of the healthy sleep habits you will learn, you will most definitely accomplish what you've set out to do; sleep train your baby and build a solid foundation for healthy sleep now and in the future.

We're all in this together. We all struggle as parents. We all hit roadblocks, face a wide variety of challenges, and often spend time comparing ourselves to others who seem to "have it all together". Now is the time to lean into these challenges and look to others for help and support. And since you're reading this, you have taken a huge step by looking for resources and reaching out for help. You might be completely sleep-deprived and desperate for help, or you're just being proactive in your sleep training efforts, but regardless of your reasoning, you will find this guide to be incredibly valuable.

As parents, we all need support. We will need support from one another now and in the future. No one has all the answers but with more information and the proper tools, you can take the first step toward sleep success. You have taken the first step to help overcome an obstacle and lead your baby and yourself to a restful night's sleep.

Chapter 1.
Understanding the Importance of Healthy Sleep

Why are healthy sleep habits important for your baby? You might be asking yourself this question. You might think to yourself that babies simply do not sleep and as a parent, that's something that you just have to accept. Society has ingrained in our brains that when you're a parent, you lose your right to sleep through the night because your child won't. Well before a baby arrives, many of us have already convinced ourselves that the nights before the baby will be the last few nights of a good night's sleep for many years to come. These thoughts alone can be incredibly detrimental and likely will cause an immense amount of anxiety and fear. We need our sleep. We rely on our sleep. Most of us look forward to sleeping and waking up feeling refreshed. When we put the thought in our head that we won't sleep again for years to come, we're just accepting what society is telling us and don't bother making an effort to change our baby's sleep habits because "this is just the way it is". This is our new reality. Well, that "reality" is a choice and does not have to be your reality. Now, that's not to say that you will always sleep the way you did before having your baby. That's not the case for a variety of reasons but, what we can do is focus on healthy sleep routines that will help our baby sleep more and for longer stretches at a time when they are developmentally ready.

When we look to science for further explanations, we know that instilling healthy habits now in our children, will have positive effects far beyond into the future. Sleep allows our minds and our bodies to rest. It allows our brain to recharge, absorb all that we learned and experienced throughout the day, and process data throughout our sleep cycle. Allowing ourselves to recharge and start fresh the next day will create a more productive day, provide more energy, and increase overall productivity. When we look at the sleep habits of children, we know that when babies and children sleep better, they are more likely to have better problem-solving abilities, make more positive decisions, encourage creativity, have more energy during the day, and develop stronger relationships with others. The list goes on. When babies sleep better, they are more likely to be less agitated during the day, they will be calmer and less anxious, and they will be able to learn things quicker because they have allowed their new little brains time to recharge and refuel.

Healthy sleep habits are not only important for your baby, but they're incredibly important for the entire family. Lack of sleep leads to many different ailments, diseases, anxiety, depression, and even obesity. This is just the shortlist. Sleep deprivation is directly linked to a variety of deficiencies. When we aren't getting the amount of sleep we need each night, we are not only putting ourselves at risk for a wide variety of problems and diseases, but we put others at risk as well. We know that our bodies absolutely, one hundred percent need sleep. We don't just need a few hours to get by. We need solid, consistent amounts of sleep each night that range anywhere from six to eight hours. The only way we are truly able to function well during the day is by getting enough sleep at night.

Science tells us that our productivity level significantly decreases with long-term sleep deprivation. How can we expect ourselves to be the best parent, employee, partner, and human being we can be when we know that by not getting enough sleep, we are not living and functioning at our full potential? We often think to ourselves that we must sacrifice many things now that we're a parent, and while yes, this can very well be true, sleep does not have to be one of the long-term sacrifices. Truly enjoying your child and embracing each moment that will quickly pass requires you to feel your best. If you aren't sleeping at night, you will not be the best parent you can be. You will be frustrated, loading up on caffeine and you might even begin to completely feel overwhelmed. Lack of sleep causes our bodies to respond negatively and without adequate sleep, we won't be able to fight back against the agitation and stress we feel. The negative reactions that can arise from sleep deprivation are not only frustrating, it can also be incredibly dangerous. When you're sleep-deprived, you're more likely to cause car accidents, fall asleep when you need to be awake and caring for your child and it might make you do something harmful that you will regret. Many human errors caused by sleep deprivation are directly linked to a variety of tragic accidents and mental breakdowns.

We often think that we can adjust to the lack of sleep that we are now facing. We think that we can learn how to get through and survive on little sleep with no side effects. Sleep deprivation is not a rite of passage for parents. It is not something that must be accepted because society tells us that we must. Research proves that getting an adequate amount of sleep is critical for our physical health, mental health, and overall quality of life. Just because you're a parent now doesn't mean that long-term sleep deprivation has to come with the territory. The common myth that parents will adjust and learn how to live with only a few hours of sleep each night is wrong. It must be understood that while the first few months can be challenging as your child will need timed feedings throughout the night, this process does not have to remain in place long-term and can be overcome when your child is ready.

We do know that in the first few months of a baby's life, they are not developmentally ready to sleep through the night. This is caused by a variety of factors. For the first three months of a baby's life, they will need to eat every three hours. Their tiny, new bellies only have room for small amounts of breastmilk or formula at a time and must be refilled every few hours. Breastmilk or formula should be your newborn's only source of nutrition in the first three months. When you add solid foods to a baby's diet around four to six months, they will be able to go longer periods without food because solids are more filling, and breastmilk and formula pass through a baby's digestive system at a rapid rate. This is why it is critical to ensure a baby is fed multiple times throughout the day and night.

In the first three months, your baby might wake up crying because they're hungry or, we might have to wake them every three hours to ensure they are getting the amount of nutrition they need. Either way, you will be losing sleep during this time while tending to the needs of your child. This is normal and necessary during this time in your child's life. However, as your baby moves through this stage and onto the next, they will no longer require this type of attention at night. Of course, as a parent, we are always aware of the happenings with our child. We are always on the lookout for when our child truly needs us. This will not go away at four months, fourteen months, or fourteen years. This will likely last a lifetime because we will never stop nurturing and caring for our children. That being said, a time will come when we must take a step back and help our children figure things out for themselves while supporting them along the way. That's exactly what will happen with sleep training. We will be there with them, encouraging, supporting, and nurturing our baby throughout the entire process. When we allow our children to figure things out on their own, such as sleeping, we are preparing them for an independent future. Now, this might seem scary for some parents because we always want our children to need us. Rest assured, that no matter what your child can do and accomplish on their own, they will always need you. They will need you well beyond childhood years and into the future. But there comes a time when we want our children to fully develop and be self-sufficient on their own. There are many long-term effects of sleep training and good sleep habits. When babies receive uninterrupted sleep, over time, this deep and meaningful sleep protects the heart against heart disease in the future. Interrupted sleep causes cortisol to elevate overnight and thus puts kids at a higher risk for heart disease and possibly even diabetes. Toddlers and babies who aren't getting enough sleep are more prone to accidents, just like adults who are sleep deprived. Many studies show that babies who aren't getting enough sleep are at a much greater risk of requiring medical attention from an injury. Attention Deficit Disorder and Attention Deficit Hyperactivity was also found to be more prevalent in children with sleep issues and often required an immense amount of intervention.

There are clear cognitive and social benefits of healthy sleep habits. We know that our moods are often linked to the amount of sleep we are getting each night. When babies aren't getting enough sleep, they might be crankier and more irritable during the day. They might have a hard time focusing or learning new things because they are constantly tired. You might even find that your baby becomes much less interested in the world around them because they are having trouble even staying awake. This can lead to a variety of frustrations felt by you, your baby, and others around you. This can also lead to developmental delays and a permanent lack of interest in people or objects due to the constant level of exhaustion your baby is feeling each day. If you want to be sure you're doing everything you can for your child to be successful in all aspects of their life, you must create a healthy, solid sleep foundation for your child to learn from and rely on. Sleep issues are much easier to combat in babies rather than trying to fix these issues later in life when your baby is much older and has completely set themselves in their ways. Facing the sleep issue head-on as early as possible will eliminate a wide variety of problems for your child in the future. It's important to be proactive and set clear guidelines on what you expect from your baby in regard to sleep.

It can be easy to feel overwhelmed by night sleep and naps. Most healthy babies will spend the majority of the twenty-four hours each day sleeping. Younger babies should be sleeping approximately fourteen to seventeen hours each day. These hours are not consecutive and will be spread out with night sleep and naps during the day. When dealing with sleep issues, feeling overwhelmed by the amount of sleep your baby needs and may or may not be getting is incredibly common. If your baby only sleeps with the support of some form of a sleep crutch, this might also be challenging as it will require a great deal of time and effort on your end. Some babies who aren't sleep trained might even have trouble sleeping in their crib or bassinet. It's very common for babies who are not able to self soothe to only be able to sleep when they are being held. For the first few months, these can be incredibly sweet and precious moments shared between parents and their baby but overtime, you might find yourself needing to work, get things done around the house, care for another child or even use the restroom- now that's a sacrifice! You might feel limited by the fact that the only way your baby will sleep is when you or someone else holds them. A great deal of pressure might even surround this time as you know your child needs to sleep but you also know other things need to get done so you find yourself conflicted and not knowing whether you should lay your baby down in their crib to cry or simply give in and hold your baby to ensure they get the sleep they greatly need. If you're like most parents, you will set your needs aside, gather the items you will need for the next two hours or so, and hold your baby so they can sleep. The younger your baby, the more naps they will need. This means that quite possibly, you are now holding your baby anywhere between six to eight hours each day, seven days a week for their nap. Keep in mind, this does not include the amount of time holding and rocking your baby to sleep at night. Your baby might even require extra hours of being held for night sleep increasing the hours of sleeping in your arms between fourteen to seventeen hours. You love your baby. Of course, you do. You rationalize what is happening by telling yourself that having to make sacrifices comes along with parenting but imagine what this is doing to your body. Not to mention your peace of mind and overall productivity level.

This mindset leads to encouraging unhealthy sleep habits and over time, your baby gets used to sleeping in your arms and now refuses to sleep anywhere else. Interesting to note, while you might think you are doing the right thing for your baby by letting them sleep in your arms, in reality, you might even be causing more harm than good as babies sleep better and move into a deeper sleep much easier when they can sleep in their own space. That's not to say that you won't ever be able to hold your baby again while they sleep but the majority of their time spent sleeping should be in their crib. Encouraging and guiding your baby to sleep in their crib is best for your baby and you. In time, the more we hold our baby, especially if we are holding them at night while we're trying to sleep as well, we can cause a great deal of damage to our bodies. If you are hunching over, keeping your arms held up, and staying in one position for too long, you will likely find yourself in pain with muscle aches and stiffness. This might even lead to interventions by a physician or quite possibly even a chiropractor. The last thing you want to feel when you are trying to be present and care for your baby is pain. Remember, encouraging healthy sleep habits will benefit you and your baby in a variety of ways. We want to ensure that you are taken care of just as well as your baby. If you want to be the best parent you can be, you must also take care of yourself, take time for yourself and be sure that you are giving your body the rest that it needs to recharge and fuel up for the next day.

Try not to feel overwhelmed during this time. Take a deep breath and know that there is a place to start to move towards healthy sleep. You will first need to start with night sleep before naps. Night sleep and day sleep involves two separate parts of the brain and must be approached separately. But before you can work on naps, we must first conquer night sleep. Although nap time would be much easier and convenient to work on first, it is clear that working on night sleep first will then lead to successful naps during the day. We will further discuss your approach to naps and how to conquer nap time in chapter ten.

Chapter 2.
The Science behind Sleep Training

Sleep training can be controversial. Often, when parents think of sleep training, they picture their child alone in their crib screaming and crying for hours on end, feeling completely helpless. The "cry it out method" is often thought to be synonymous with any form of sleep training. The negativity and association that surrounds sleep training often prevents parents who need help the most to partake in any sort of program that might very well help their child sleep at night. Parents often associate sleep training with strict parenting styles. While it can be easy to quickly disregard any form of sleep training out of fear and guilt, it is important to remember the many different programs and options that are available for you and your child. Are some of these programs a bit more extreme? Yes. Are these strict programs the only options for sleep training? Absolutely not. There are a variety of ways to sleep train your child. You can even customize your plan based on different program elements that you wish to include. Now, that's not to say there won't be some crying involved. Babies cry that's a fact and a part of parenting. There will be times with any effective program that will involve your baby crying but that doesn't mean that you won't be there, right alongside them as their most supportive cheerleader. You can and should let your child know that you are there for them should they truly need you. We will get into the strategy behind this in chapter eight but for now, please remember that sleep training can be done in many different ways with minimal crying involved.

Once you learn how to identify the different reasons behind your baby crying, you will be able to better care for them and you will know when you're needed. Once you sleep train your baby, you will truly know when something is wrong, and your child needs your help. It will be much easier to differentiate a true need from a normal yelp or quick cry while your child sleeps. Before you follow any sleep training program, whether it be this program or another, you must first understand the science behind sleep training, how it works, and why it's truly important for your child. There isn't a specific amount of time that's right or wrong for your baby to cry throughout the process. Only you will know when to intervene, but we will give you basic steps that you can follow to get you on your way to sleep-filled nights. You, as your child's parent, will be the best one to make the call on when to step in. Many people think that you must let your child cry for an hour, two hours, some even think ten minutes will suffice. The truth is, only you know. Only you will know the right amount of time. You will know what feels right to you and what your comfort level is. All sleep training, especially this sleep training guide can be customized depending on your comfort level and what will work best for your baby. If you try this program, step-by-step for at least the first week and you find that it simply isn't working for your baby, feel free to customize as you see fit. You are in charge of making sleep training your own and making it fit your circumstances and threshold. With that said, before giving up a program, please ensure that you have truly tried your very best to make the program work for your baby. Putting in the time and effort necessary is the most important step for any program to be successful.

Common Myths

A common myth is that growth spurts are to blame for your child's sleep issues. Parents often think that growth spurts are at the root of your baby not getting an adequate amount of sleep. This is a myth. It's important to note that growth spurts only last about a week, not months at a time. Along with growth spurts being to blame for sleep troubles, another common myth is that babies need extra calories and they're waking up because they need to eat every hour or two. While it is true that babies do need to increase their caloric intake at times, this does not mean that a healthy baby should need to be up every hour to eat. If this is happening with your baby, the likely cause is that your child has now formed a habit and is waking up because they're familiar with the process. When we give into feeding our baby every hour or two throughout the night, the baby then begins to rely on this routine and in turn, is unable to fall asleep without support.

The clear facts on sleep training show us there are many different ways to sleep train. There are views on each program, and you must decide on the program that best aligns with your comfort level and beliefs. The sleep training approach that is described below is a combination of a variety of programs that leads to successful sleep with minimal crying involved. Regardless of the program you choose, it's important to note that pediatricians recommend sleep training your baby. There is a reason for this. Pediatricians are aware of the incredible benefits of sleep training and highly recommend that parents partake in a program if their baby isn't sleeping well. At every well-baby visit, you will commonly be asked how your baby is sleeping at night. Answer this question honestly. Having an honest conversation with your doctor will enable your doctor to provide helpful resources and tips you might be able to follow and lean on.

Types of Sleep

There are two types of sleep for babies: quiet and active. Babies are difficult to wake during quiet sleep and sleep very light during active sleep. When your baby is grunting, groaning, and fighting their swaddle, they are in the quiet stage of sleep. It is very common for parents to pick up their babies during this time because they think they are struggling and need support when they are just sleeping in a light stage. When a baby is in the quiet stage of sleep, they will wake up frequently throughout the night. You might not realize it, but you also wake up frequently and check your surroundings throughout the night. We don't realize that we do this because we know how to put ourselves back to sleep without even realizing we were awake, even if it was only for a few seconds. The difference is that when babies do this, they don't know how to put themselves back to sleep and then, begin to cry out for help. It often takes time for a baby to develop this skill. With sleep training, we are slowly teaching our baby to learn this skill and be able to put themselves back to sleep when they wake up throughout the night just like we do as adults.

Sleep Regressions

At month four, a common myth tells us that sleep issues are caused by a four-month sleep regression. Sleep regressions are often to blame for sleep troubles. It's important to note that while your baby is going through developmental and physical changes that does not mean that they shouldn't be able to sleep well. It does however mean that sleep is vital for your baby to properly develop and grow. By month four, your baby has officially entered into infancy and has now moved beyond the newborn stage. Cognitive and physical development is advancing at a rapid and exciting rate! It might feel as though time is flying by. That tends to happen when we are happy, busy, and enjoying our new families. Each new stage will come quicker than the last and before you know it, your baby will soon be a toddler. But before then, we want to ensure your baby has the tools it needs to be a successful sleeper. We also want to ensure that you, as parents, also have the resources you need to train your baby and to support one another along with your baby through this exciting and sometimes frustrating path.

Your baby has now entered into a new developmental stage. Growth and major changes will be experienced by your baby at a rapid rate in the coming months. During this time, your baby begins to realize they are part of the world. This realization is exciting! Now that your baby is starting to recognize that every action causes a reaction, it is a good time to start forming healthy habits and routines for your baby. Establishing a clear and predictable bedtime for your baby will not only ensure it knows what comes next but they will begin to follow along with the routine the more it is performed. At this stage, babies begin to understand patterns and can understand that after our bedtime bath comes our bedtime story, and then a massage and onto a nursing session. Whatever your routine may be, your baby will begin the process of being prepared for the inevitable outcome, sleep.

There will be factors that change the way your baby sleeps or interfere with healthy sleep patterns as it grows through different stages but sleep regressions should not be blamed for these obstacles. When we tell ourselves that our baby is going through something that can't be avoided, such as a sleep regression, we give in to these myths and are less likely to take a step toward making a change. We give in and tell ourselves that there's nothing we can do until it passes through this regression and then the next. We settle for this fate instead of fully understanding the actions that we can take to improve sleep habits. It's easier to settle for an obstacle rather than working to overcome and make a change for the better. Sleep training will not be easy, but it will be worth it. As you move through the process of sleep training, remember the facts around baby sleep, and do not let yourself or your partner fall into these traps and myths. Giving in to these myths will only contribute to unhealthy sleep habits and prolong them for an even longer period. Making a change takes strength but remember, you're a parent, you can get through anything! Especially if it is truly best for your baby.

Babies are like adults and have different variations of sleep stages they move throughout the night. It's important to understand these stages of sleep to better understand the needs of your baby. The first stage your baby moves through involves droopy eyes and drowsiness. This is the best time to put your baby down, alone in their crib for the night. You always want to make sure your baby is drowsy but still awake when you remove yourself from the nursery. The second stage is very light sleep. During this stage, your baby might startle, move, or even make noises. It can be very tempting to want to pick your baby up during this time, especially if this is your first and you haven't heard nighttime baby grunts before. It can absolutely sound like your baby is awake but rest assured, your baby is sleeping during this time, and picking your baby up will only make it harder for your baby to fall asleep on their own over time. We want to avoid negative sleep habits before they start. Ensuring that you let your child sleep during stage 2 on their own is vital. Then comes stage three, this is the sleep stage when your baby is quiet and in a deep sleep. Followed by stage four, even deeper sleep for your baby. If you're like most parents, you might even touch your child or want to pick them up during this time to make sure it is ok and breathing. Please, do not pick up your baby when it is in deep sleep. If you must check them for your peace of mind, gently rest your hand quietly on your baby's stomach and you will feel slow movements from their belly. It is very normal to want this reassurance as a new parent and one who cares greatly about your sweet baby. There are special devices and monitors available should you need extra peace of mind while your baby sleeps. These might be a good option if you find yourself constantly wanting to go in and check on your baby even if you have a baby monitor on hand and functioning. These devices can track your child's breathing patterns and heartbeat and can easily be linked to an app on your phone. Please keep in mind that most of these devices have not been FDA approved but many parents do find them incredibly helpful and comforting during a time when your life can sometimes feel incredibly chaotic.

Chapter 3.
Preparing to Sleep Train your Baby

Before beginning any sleep training program, always check with your pediatrician to ensure your baby is developmentally and physically ready to begin a sleep training program. Some babies need extra support throughout the night and leaving them to self-soothe and put themselves to sleep might not be best for those children. During any sleep training program, your child must be physically ready to go long periods, approximately six to eight hours without a feeding. As your child continues to grow and move through the sleep training process, they will be able to sleep much longer periods at a time. By the time your child is four months old, they should be able to sleep between six to eight hours each night with one-night feeding. Imagine that? Keep this in mind as you prepare for sleep training. You can sleep through just about the entire night right along with your child. You will be able to sleep even longer the older your baby is. The middle of the night feedings will mostly stop, and you won't be rocking your child back to sleep at 1:00 AM. An example of this sleep schedule would be putting your child to sleep between 7:00 PM to 8:00 PM and ensuring your child sleeps until at least 6:00 AM each night with one-night feeding. Most likely, this night feeding will be a dream feed. We will discuss dream feeding your baby in chapter seven. This might seem like a distant reality for you now but rest assured, over time, your child will be able to sleep long stretches at a time without requiring support from you at night.

Children with certain health issues might need to wait until they are a bit older before they can truly follow a sleep training program.

Your pediatrician will be able to guide a time frame that fits the needs of your child. Rule out any underlying health issues before starting a sleep training program. Babies are susceptible to many different developmental changes and medical conditions that might be impacting their sleep. Teething, food allergies, reflux, and even sleep apnea are conditions that may be impacting your child and the amount they're physically able to sleep at night. Babies who have been born prematurely are also highly susceptible to these conditions and might not be physically ready to sleep train at four months. It might take them a bit longer to be ready and able to participate in a program. Be sure to have your child thoroughly checked by their pediatrician before embarking on the sleep training journey. Most babies are ready to sleep train once they reach four months. If your baby has been given the stamp of sleep training approval from your pediatrician, it's time to make a list of how you can best prepare for sleep training. You don't just flick a switch and begin training your child. This isn't something that can or should happen quickly without truly understanding what needs to be prepared beforehand. Many factors come to play with any program, especially a sleep training program.

Before starting any sleep training, it's important that you psychologically prepare yourself to train your baby. Sit down with your partner and truly discuss if you are both ready to fully commit to this program. This is a time to come together and truly build on your existing partnership. It's time to lean on one another for support and love. Parenting can be difficult. It can also take a toll on your partnership and create obstacles. It is important to be proactive, have honest conversations with one another about how you're feeling, and ensure you are both on the same page before you begin. Remind each other throughout the program why you started and work hard not to take your frustrations out on one another. This program will only improve your partnership and remind you of the strong bond and partnership that you share. Being mindful and aware of these potential obstacles ahead of time will ensure that you are as prepared as possible for what's to come. Before the program, we might feel completely fine and free of stress and anxiety but throughout, this could very well change. On the flip side, you might feel strong and diligent in getting through the program. Either way, you want to be prepared for both scenarios.

It takes a village to raise a child and sleep training is an avenue that you will need support when embarking on this journey. You must ask yourself if you are ready to commit the time and make the effort to follow the program in full. It's easy for parents to fall back into old habits for short-term benefits. Most likely, you have been able to put your baby to sleep by using some form of a crutch to do so. A sleep crutch can be anything from rocking, bouncing, and nursing until your child falls completely to sleep.

When parents aren't fully ready to commit to the program, they often revert to their old ways and use whatever tool that has worked for them in the past, even if the results are short-term. We do this out of desperation. We do this because sleep deprivation makes us do illogical things and at the moment, the quick fix to put your baby back to sleep is often utilized. We've all been there. It's 2:00 AM on the first night of your sleep training program. Remember, you started this program with the best intentions and the intent to remain consistent. You have finally fallen into a deep sleep and suddenly, your baby begins to cry. You lay in bed hoping and praying that they will go back to sleep on their own. You look to the monitor and see no end in sight. Your baby is crying so loud that you simply can't ignore it. You're exhausted, emotionally, and physically. You know that if you don't get enough sleep tonight, your productivity level at work tomorrow will be non-existent. Not to mention the presentation you have to make at 9:00 AM. Time goes on and your baby is still crying. You decide that the best solution at this point is for you to get up, pick up your baby, and use whatever crutch necessary to get your baby back to sleep. You finally get your baby back to sleep and go back to bed but only to be woken up again at

3:30 AM, 5:00 AM, and 5:45 AM. Each time, you find yourself dragging yourself back into your baby's room to do whatever it takes to put them back to sleep. After the last crying session, you fall back to sleep at 6:00 AM but only to be woken up again by your alarm at 6:30 AM. You wake up feeling completely exhausted and disappointed in yourself for not following through with the sleep training program you initially committed to. You feel ashamed that instead of pushing through during the necessary training time, you fell back into old habits due to pure exhaustion which means, you weren't fully ready and committed to dedicating the time and work into this program. You tell yourself that tonight will be different. You're exhausted but prepared and committed because something needs to change. You are desperate for sleep and now, you're ready.

Once you've mentally prepared yourself for the task at hand, it's important to remember to remain calm and consistent throughout the process. Sleep training your baby will bring up a host of feelings and emotions. You might feel guilty, emotional and you might even feel as though you're a bad parent. When you're feeling this way, tell yourself how much better your baby will feel if they are sleeping better at night. Think about the joy that will come back into your life once you're no longer sleep deprived. Remember that as parents, we sometimes have to make difficult decisions that will lead to positive outcomes for our family. Keep your eye on the prize and your heart on the positive outcomes of sleep training. Remaining calm and consistent will ensure that you will also remain consistent. You might need to bring in reinforcement to ensure that you can keep yourself focused and consistent. Parents might choose to pull out a good book, put on a show, or maybe even have a glass of wine. Identify ways to keep yourself calm before starting the program so you're not scrambling once your baby begins to cry. This will not only cause stress and anxiety, but it might even make you stop the program. The more that you can prepare yourself for the process, the more successful you will be.

Remaining calm throughout the program is important for yourself and your baby. Babies pick up on our emotions. They can feel when something is off or if someone is anxious. They are tiny sponges that often absorb the emotions we show them. If we remain calm, it will encourage our baby to feel calm as well. While it's easy to feel stress and anxiety during this time for a variety of reasons, the more diligent we can be about remaining calm and consistent, the better the outcome will be for mom, dad and baby. If certain parts of the training cause an immense amount of stress and uneasy emotions, and you feel that you might not be able to push through without intervening, designate your partner to control that part of the program. Try taking a walk, exercising, reading a book, or doing something in another room where you can decompress and allow your partner to handle the point in the program that is difficult for you. This doesn't mean that your partner is the one in charge of sleep training, this just allows for a balance of the situation. Be mindful of your pressure points and ask for help when needed but remember, this program relies on a solid partnership to achieve success. This is not a time to remove yourself completely from the situation. You will both need to be involved and be able to rely on one another throughout the program. Being open and honest with your partner during this time will not only be helpful for your baby but also for your partnership as well. Sleep deprivation and disturbances can cause an immense amount of stress for families. Be sure that you continue working on your partnership during this time and keep your bond tight.

In preparing for sleep training, you must rely on a strong support system, even if that system only includes your partner, to help you through this time. If you are willing to step outside of your immediate circle of support, you might find that joining a sleep training and/or parent support group will be helpful in sleep training. Having the support of other parents who are going through some of the same struggles can not only be reassuring, but you might even gain new insight into other ways parents are approaching sleep training. Learning from others and sharing ideas is a great way for parents to connect, feel support, and gain inspiration for new parenting styles. You might even gain a new sense of confidence when it comes to your parenting skills when you receive positive feedback from other parents. Other parents might even want to mimic some of your parenting skills! Connect, share ideas, and support other parents on this journey. These support groups can focus on many different topics and you might find them helpful long after you've successfully sleep trained your baby. Many parents who join parent groups even find long-lasting friends along the way! Remember that sleep training and parenting is not a solo mission, regardless of what your unique situation looks like, you will always be able to find others in the community who will be there to support you along the way.

You've received the all-clear from your pediatrician, you have joined a parent group for support, you even have identified a way to track your child's sleep data, now you need to identify the right time to begin this program. You will want to be sure that you begin a sleep training program at the best possible time. Avoid beginning a program just after an illness, during an intense period of teething, and just after a vacation or any event that changed your child's normal routine. Clearing your calendar is also a must! This comes along with identifying the right time to begin any sleep training program. If there are changes in your schedule such as working late, an upcoming dinner party, or even guests visiting from out of town that might not be the best time to begin training. Be sure that you can be present during the time needed for sleep training. You don't want your child to be thrown off by inconsistency and feel that the routine is off. Will the routine change overtime? Most likely, yes. But during sleep training, you want to do everything you possibly can to ensure your child's routine and all those who will be helping. These circumstances might make the program even more challenging as your undivided attention is critical to achieving success. For example, if there are others in your household, they might have their views on sleep training and could even prevent you from beginning the program altogether.

   Keeping a record of sleep training progress might also be helpful and will keep you focused. You will also be able to see data on the progress you and your baby will be making throughout the program. The record can be kept by using a downloadable free template or simply writing down information in a journal. You might even want to look back at the information one day when you sleep train your next baby. Or, this could also be a great addition to a baby book. But whatever you choose to do with the data found throughout the program, keeping a record will keep you consistent and prepared to move through each day of the program. It might even give you something to look forward to. An example of your journal entry might look something like this:

May 5, 2020

> *Night five of sleep training. Baby Joey was put to bed at 7:30 PM. He was nursed at 7:00 PM for ten minutes and fell asleep by 8:05 PM.*

> *Baby Joey woke up at 11:30 PM, cried for fifteen minutes before putting himself back to sleep. Mama went into baby Joey's room at 12:15 AM to dream feed him for seven minutes. Baby Joey stayed asleep and was placed back in his crib by 12:22 AM.*

> *Baby Joey slept the rest of the night and woke up at 7:00 AM!*

   Even if you initially thought you might not be the type of person who would journal, now might be the time to start. Remember, journaling and keeping data and the progress your family will be making is critical. Find what feels right to you and what works best for your family. There's no right or wrong way to prepare but the more resources you have available, the more likely you will be to find success. If journaling or manually keeping track of your child's sleep data isn't for you. There are numerous options of apps you can easily download that will help you keep track of all of your baby's developments. These apps are often recommended for the first few months with your newborn as they will help you keep track of regular diaper changes, feedings, naps, and other developmental changes. This data is important during your well-baby visits and can be easily pulled from the app once you visit your pediatrician. Most apps can also be accessed by both parents and make it easy to link information inputted by both parents. Access to experts may also be available with paid subscriptions along with other helpful benefits. Again, this is not a requirement but a helpful tool that might support your sleep training program. Downloading these apps ahead of time will give you access to resources available and will likely provide helpful information that will support you along this journey.

Identifying ways to prepare your baby for sleep training is incredibly important. You first want to be sure that your baby is getting enough feedings throughout the day so it is less hungry at night. We want to fill up the engine throughout the day so there are no pit stops at night. Your baby might not be interested in eating because the world around them is now incredibly exciting. They are beginning to move into a new phase of understanding and being aware of their surroundings. Their eyes are beginning to focus and their brain is starting to make connections with what's around them. The world is incredibly stimulating, especially for a new baby who is experiencing life for the very first time. Every color, object, sound, and smell is new for them. While it tries to make sense of it all and make connections with what's in front of them, they simply do not have time to eat. They are a busy baby! We, as parents and caregivers need to make time for our baby to eat and place them in an environment that is in a sense boring and not very exciting to ensure our child eats an adequate amount free from distractions.

Most likely, if you're preparing to sleep train, your baby is at an age when it is not only curious but is now more aware of people and objects that fall within their line of sight. As their vision develops and they can see their parents, toys and all the new colors they couldn't see before. The world around them is now intriguing and very distracting. How can you expect your baby to focus on eating when they are busy absorbing all the things around them?

To ensure your baby is getting enough feedings throughout the day, be sure to remove them from a stimulating environment for daytime feedings. Be sure the room it is feeding in is quiet and free from distractions. You don't want your baby so distracted throughout the day and not eating enough. You will most definitely find that it requires feeding sessions in the middle of the night if this is the case. Doing what you can ahead of time to ensure proper feedings occur during the day will greatly impact the length of time your baby will be able to sleep at night. We want to ensure your baby has a full tummy from their meals throughout the day and is not crying in the middle of the night because it truly is hungry. Keeping a log of the amount of time your baby feeds and when, will be helpful to properly track and look back on data. If you're concerned that your child is not eating enough, ask your pediatrician to provide advice. You might need to change your diet if your breastfeeding or change formulas to ensure the necessary number of calories are consumed by your baby during the day. We want to focus on timed, consistent feedings to ensure your baby doesn't need to nurse or bottle-feed every hour. To ensure proper feedings take place throughout the day, you also want to make sure your baby doesn't fall asleep or begin to drift off during feeding sessions. If needed, lightly caress the cheek of your baby to keep them awake. This will help them to not startle but will keep them from falling asleep. You will also want to offer more feedings during the day. Like adults, daytime is the time for them to eat and we want to ensure they associate the day with eating and gradually eliminate this from their middle of the night routine. Try offering your baby a feeding every two hours even if they do not seem hungry or if they recently had a feeding. This will encourage them to eat more often throughout the day and fill up their tummy, so they are not hungry at night. We want to ensure that if your baby is crying at night, it isn't out of necessity.

Now let's take a look at what you can expect once you begin sleep training. You can first expect that your emotions might be up and down. You will likely hit highs and lows throughout the process. You might even continue to question whether or not you've made the right decision to begin this program. If you begin feeling this way, take a moment and try to remember why you started the program in the first place. It might be helpful to utilize your journal and write down all the reasons sleep training is a good fit for your family before you even begin. That way, when times get difficult, you can refer back to what you wrote and remember why you started in the first place. Be sure to write out what sleep will do for your family so you will also be mindful of the outcome. Parents often feel guilty about sleep training because of the negative reputation it has been given. The reality is that a sleep training program that best fits your family, is incredibly beneficial. Keep that in mind if you begin to struggle with the process. There might be some tears involved, and anger toward your partner for some reason because this is what stress does to us. Try and remember to take a step back and breathe. Remember that as long as your baby has been fed, burped, and changed, your child is likely crying because they want you to put them to sleep, they do not need you to put them to sleep. There is a difference here.

You can also expect some crying to be involved. Before you tell yourself there's no way you can sit back and listen to your baby crying before stepping in, remember that to make anything change, there might be difficult obstacles involved. For sleep training, one of the biggest obstacles that you will likely face is listening to your baby cry. Remember, babies cry for many different reasons, it doesn't always mean they are in pain or desperately need their parents. Sometimes they cry because their routine has changed, and something is happening that hasn't happened before. When your routine changes, do you ever feel out of sorts? Do you ever want to squeal a bit and say, hey wait a minute, this is different! What's happening? Why are things changing? Where will this lead? Of course, you do. That's the normal reaction that anyone would have when something changes or feels different than it did before. For babies going through a sleep training program, not having their mother nurse them to sleep every night is a big change. When their dad isn't bouncing them on yoga ball until they fall asleep, this too is a change, and this might lead to crying. The only way for a baby to truly learn how to self-soothe themselves to sleep is to let them cry for a bit. Now, this doesn't mean that you won't be there with them. You will be able to go into their room and comfort your baby after some time passes. We will get into the details around this in chapter seven.

Chapter 4.
Creating a Sleep Friendly Environment

Now that you've taken all the appropriate steps to prepare yourself, your family and your baby for sleep training, it's time to ensure that your house and your baby's room is conducive for healthy sleep. Before we fall asleep, we look for sleep cues to get our mind and body ready for sleep. We look for darkness, quiet places, and serene atmospheres. Our baby requires the same surroundings as they prepare for sleep. If the room is loud, bright, and chaotic, we may find it difficult to fall asleep or even relax. There's a reason why people who live in quiet, suburban areas rate their sleep efficiency higher than those who live in loud cities like New York and Chicago. For most, loud noise makes it almost impossible to sleep. We look for peaceful, relaxing spaces to put our minds at rest for the night. Studies show that even doing something as simple as leaving the television on all night greatly impacts our quality of sleep. Outside noise prohibits us from getting the deep and peaceful sleep that we so greatly need. At this time, you will also need to examine the room where your child will sleep from a variety of angles. One, you will want to fix any creaky floors or doors that might be squeaking. Keep in mind that babies are very sensitive to sound and they will easily hear small noises like a creaking door when you enter or exit the room. You will be glad that you fixed anything in the room that might have caused unnecessary noise from time to time. Then, you will want to ensure the room is clean and organized. A room that is cluttered and chaotic is not conducive to sleep and will potentially prevent your baby from sleeping well throughout the night. Getting organized ahead of time will also help you to find things that you need quickly and will create an environment with less stress. Organizing, labeling, and placing items in easy to reach places that you will frequently be accessing will be very helpful as you care for your baby. If you are working to organize your baby's room, remember, the nursery is used for a variety of things and proper organization will help you to access items without feeling overwhelmed or stressed. Organizing will also make for a smoother transition at night for your baby. You will know exactly where to find your sleep cues and props without having to stress over lost items when it's time to put your baby down to sleep. Organizing, cleaning, and creating a peaceful sleep environment can also be done by incorporating items that you feel are relaxing. Himalayan salt lamps, dream catchers, family photos, and comfortable blankets are all peaceful items that can be included in your baby's room. Get creative and think about the items that bring you peace. These items are likely to bring your baby a great deal of peace as well.

When creating the most peaceful sleep setting for your baby, you want to first identify where your child will be sleeping. Depending on the age of your baby, they might still be sleeping in your room as many parents choose to sleep with their child in their room until they reach twelve months. If you choose to keep your child in your room, it is recommended that during sleep training, you and your partner sleep in another room. This may be difficult for you given that you have likely slept next to your baby every night for the last four-plus months but, removing yourself from your child's space will provide for the best possible sleep outcome. Please know that sleeping somewhere else during this time does not have to be long-term, you are welcome to move back into your room with your baby once you've completed the training. It is recommended that parents sleep somewhere else during this time for a variety of reasons. For one, if you're a nursing mother, your baby will be able to smell your breast milk. If your baby knows that milk is close by, they will be more inclined to cry and want to nurse than they would be if it is unable to smell your scent. Have you ever been somewhere and smelled something delicious and immediately felt hungry even if you just ate? This also happens to your baby. Milk is comforting, nurturing, and fulfilling for your baby. Nursing not only fills up their tummy but this is also their way of feeling connected to their mother. If your baby senses that you're there and hasn't completed the sleep training program, they might be more inclined to wake up and need your support. This is what we want to avoid as much as possible while sleep training. This doesn't mean that your baby won't want to nurse anymore, and it doesn't mean that they won't still cry out from time to time for you at night. It means that during the time that they are sleep training, they will learn how to comfort and calm themselves instead of relying on their parents to comfort them back to sleep each time they wake up.

We may not realize but we could very well be keeping our baby up at night. If you are constantly moving, adjusting, or even getting up to use the restroom in the middle of the night, your baby most likely hears every move you make and then wakes up. If you or your partner tends to snore or talk in your sleep, this can also be interfering with your child's sleep. Remember, the different sleep cycles your baby moves through each night involves times of very light sleep taking place. When your child is in the light sleep stage, they can easily be disturbed and will likely hear your snoring, moving, or adjusting at night when it is trying to sleep peacefully. With that said, your baby might be keeping you up as well. When your child is close, you are much more likely to constantly want to place your hand on your child to make sure they are ok. You might hear them moving, grunting, or making other normal noises in their sleep and wake up constantly to check on them. You might even be more inclined to pick your child up if they are crying in the middle of the night if they're sleeping close to you. These are all factors that can not only interrupt your sleep but your baby's sleep as well. If you do choose to keep your baby in your room, for the time being, the best thing you can do is move their crib or bassinet as far away from your bed as possible. Doing this will allow them to have their own space and they will be less likely to see you, smell your scent or hear you if you're tossing around at night. That being said, it is very common for parents to feel that it is best to change their child's sleep environment and one of the main reasons parents choose to move their baby into their own room before the American Pediatric Association recommendation of one year. While the APA recommends waiting until one year to move your child into their own room due to SIDS (Sudden Infant Death Syndrome), there are steps that you can take to keep your baby safe in their own room.

Many parents who move their child into their own room are comforted by knowing they can see their baby on the monitor throughout the night. They know they will be able to hear them if it cries and can take a look to see what the situation truly looks like. Some parents might have needed an extra level of comfort and choose to purchase devices that can either be worn by the baby throughout the night or can be placed under their mattress. These devices monitor your baby's heart and oxygen levels to ensure that everything is well throughout the night. They work by either tracking your baby's movement throughout the night or their pulse and oxygen levels by being wrapped around your baby's foot like a small sock. This data is sent to an app and will alert you if the data moves to a dangerous level such as an elevated heart rate or lower oxygen percentage. This data also shows your child's sleep patterns and when it wakes up at night. It's important to note that often these devices have glitches and might go off in the middle of the night even if nothing is wrong. If you choose to purchase a device for your baby, be sure to read the entire user's manual along with what to expect. This will ensure that you are prepared if the alarm goes off when it's not supposed to and how to avoid that from happening altogether.

The fear of something happening to your baby in the middle of the night is one of the most impactful reasons why parents do not choose to sleep train their baby. They truly feel that if they leave their baby alone, to put themselves to sleep that something could happen to them. This common fear felt by many parents can be debilitating and it can also prevent you and your baby from getting the sleep you desperately need. This fear not only prevents parents from sleep training their baby, but it can also cause a great deal of stress and anxiety. If you are constantly thinking about something bad happening, you are more likely to feel overwhelmed and unable to make the best decisions for your baby. You will end up doing whatever it takes to make sure your baby is ok even when they're completely fine. You might even find yourself hovering over your child's crib all night just in case something happens. While it is normal to be worried about your child and want to ensure they're always taken care of, we don't want our fears to override what is best for our baby and prevent us from making decisions that will help our children now and well into the future. For parents who need an added layer of comfort and peace of mind, some devices will put your mind at ease and will help you take a step in making the best decision for your baby. Remember, as your child grows, these feelings will most likely change, and you will get stronger. For many parents, the fear of SIDS can completely overrule their decision-making abilities. As a parent, if you are constantly thinking and being fearful about SIDS, you might even find that you end up not being able to enjoy your baby as much as you would otherwise. These fears can impact the way we live, the way we parent and, the amount of sleep that we get or don't get. For some, staying up all night with their baby is easier than sleep training and having to constantly worry about something happening to their baby in the middle of the night. With that said, purchasing devices like the one mentioned can be a great way to know that you can monitor your baby throughout the night through this device and also on the baby monitor. While these devices have not been FDA approved, they are in high demand and can cost a pretty penny. Most of the time parents are willing to trust a device that even partially works if it provides some extra comfort and peace of mind. Identify what you think will help you through sleep training and make sure that you have these devices and items ready before you begin the program.

When preparing the best sleep environment for your baby, you will want to be mindful of the temperature in their room. Keeping your baby's room at a cool temperature is recommended and encourages a safe and effective space for sleep. You will want to make sure that your baby isn't too warm or too hot as this will lead to them feeling uncomfortable and will also potentially lead to tears. Keep in mind that we are working to eliminate all possible scenarios that might create an uncomfortable environment for your baby that could very well lead to them getting upset and reaching out for your attention. If you think about how you sleep, you will be able to keep what you need in mind when creating this space for your baby. Babies are just tiny humans that sleep very similarly to how we do as adults. If being too hot or too cold makes you uncomfortable when you sleep, this will very possibly be the same for your baby. With the recommended sleep temperature for a baby's room being 68 to 72 degrees, you will likely need a few items that will help achieve this temperature. For starters, you will need a thermostat in your baby's room. Before running out to buy one, check your baby monitor as many monitors tend to also track the temperature of your baby's room. Once you identify the current temperature, you will need to see if the room is too hot or too cool and what needs to potentially be brought in. You might need to install a fan in your baby's room if it's too hot. Your focus should be on trying to keep their room cool rather than warm. You can always add extra light layers onto your baby if needed but keeping their room cool is not only recommended for healthy sleep but also safety. SIDS (Sudden Infant Death Syndrome), every parent's worst nightmare has been linked to babies overheating. While many other factors have been linked to this heartbreaking syndrome, it is important to be aware of the potential risks around keeping your child overly bundled or the heat too high. Installing a ceiling fan is usually a good idea and has been known to help avoid SIDS by keeping the air around your baby constantly circulating. A good rule of thumb is following how you feel in a room. If you think the room is too hot or too cold, your baby will likely feel the same way. There is a common misconception with new babies that they are constantly cold and need to be bundled up. If you touch your baby's fingers and they are cold, this is normal as long as their chest is warm. Feeling your baby's cold fingers can be concerning and lead to bundling up your baby. Keep in mind that this is normal when the rest of his body is warm. Parents should always use good judgment and follow how they are dressed during the day and for sleep and if anything, might need to add a light onesie under your baby's clothes but other than that, you should dress your baby the way that you are dressed for the day and the weather.

Whether you choose to sleep in another room while your baby stays in yours, or your baby is continuing to sleep in its nursery, you will want to install a baby monitor. Baby monitors are a great way to keep an eye on your baby at night and while it naps during the day. You will be able to hear if it cries or truly needs you to come in for them. During sleep training, this is a great way to give you the peace of mind that you might need throughout the process. You will be able to visually see that your baby is ok and is crying because they can't put themselves back to sleep just yet. This should bring you peace of mind that you need to keep moving through the program. Knowing that you can see exactly what they are doing, how they are positioned, if their onesie is falling off and when it falls asleep successful, will be critical. A sleep monitor can be installed in one room and moved to another if and when you choose to move your baby to their nursery. Keep in mind that monitors can range in price but as long as you can see and hear your baby, the added features are simply added benefits. If you choose, you can even buy two monitors and keep one in your child's room and the other you could use if you travel, go to grandma's house or visit with friends when your baby needs to take a nap. Monitors are helpful for parents and there are a variety of options that can be purchased. Some monitors link with some of the devices mentioned above that help track your baby's movements, heart rate, and oxygen levels at night.

Once your camera is installed and working properly, you will want to make sure that your baby's room is dark. This is not always as easy as turning off the light in their room. One of the best ways to get your baby to sleep on their own is to ensure the room is as dark as it can be. At this age, babies are not afraid of the dark and are unable to process this concept. If you're concerned the room might be too dark for your baby, remember that a dark room mimics the darkness of a womb, where they lived for over nine months. Darkness encourages healthy, deep sleep for babies and is also a sleep cue for your child. When it sees that the room is completely dark, it will trigger its memory of falling asleep and it will associate the darkness with sleepy time. Many rooms are not necessarily set up for this type of darkness and you might find yourself buying blackout drapes, putting up trash bags, or finding other ways to truly make the room as dark as it can be. Any bit of light that comes through can very well prohibit your baby from sleeping. You want to make sure that each window in the room is completely covered, most likely they will need to be covered with dark blackout curtains. Parents often choose to use two sets of curtains or extra blackout coverings behind the curtains when putting their baby down for sleep. Remember, any ray of light will trigger the thought of being awake and playing when they should be thinking that it's time to fall asleep. Keep in mind that you want to darken your baby's room without overheating it. This is why it's important to track the temperature of the room to see if you need fans to ensure the appropriate temperature is reached. When you darken a room, it often brings heat and this will need to be monitored over time, specifically, in the summer months. Be mindful of this time of the year and be careful not to overdress your baby in the summer. You will need to change out their pajamas once the weather changes and transition to lightweight options for them. A good rule of thumb, when you begin wearing lighter pajamas, most likely, it's time to change your baby's as well.

Chapter 5.
Sleep Safety, Sleep Props and Swaddling

Before you begin the program, you must follow all sleep guidelines to ensure the location where your baby will sleep is safe and secure. To start, you want to be sure that your baby is either sleeping in a crib or a bassinet. If your baby is sleeping in a crib, be sure to put your child's crib mattress at the lowest possible setting. Depending on the age and size of your baby, you will be able to determine the best baby bed that currently fits their needs. They will grow and their bed will change over time but for now, you want to focus on the best place for them to sleep over the next few weeks and months. Some parents often choose to avoid a bassinet all together while others choose to start with a bassinet and then transition to a larger crib when your baby is ready.

Now that you've identified the best bed for your baby to sleep train, you will need to make sure it's safe. Check the crib according to the manual and ensure that it's sturdy and that all of the screws and loose items on the crib are tightly fastened. Your baby's crib should be checked frequently to ensure nothing is loose and it is free of loose pieces that could be a choking hazard. Your baby's bed should also be free of any loose items placed in the crib. Bumpers, pillows, and blankets are suffocation hazards for babies and should not be placed in your child's crib. The crib should be fitted with a tight sheet and nothing more. At this age, babies are often unable to roll themselves over and might find themselves stuck in a position with a blanket or pillow and they might not be able to get themselves out of this position. The best way to ensure it is safe in its crib at night is to eliminate all extra items. Avoid toys, anti-roll pillows, and sleep positioners as these items could lead to choking or suffocation. You will also want to be sure the space around the crib is free from wires or chords that might be within reach of your child. If you choose to use a monitor, be sure the cord is not within reach as these often hang down from the ceiling where the camera is placed and can be a hazard for your baby. Be mindful of what's around the crib and anything the baby would be able to reach if it sticks its hand through the crib. Remember, babies are curious creatures and want to touch and feel anything that might be around them. To ensure they do not do anything that would present a hazard, clear the area around the crib completely. Bring your partner in to examine the space to ensure that an extra set of eyes can review the space and catch anything you might have missed.

Since you won't be using blankets to keep your baby warm, you might want to consider swaddling your baby if it is still aged appropriate or utilizing a sleep sack or wearable blanket to keep them warm throughout the night. If you are swaddling your baby, and the are at least four months old, it's time to stop swaddling its arms down. This is the time when it will learn to fall asleep with its arms outside of the swaddle. Try pulling one arm out of the swaddle at a time to get them used to sleep without their arms swaddled down. At this age, your child will begin to roll over and you need to be sure their arms are free to ensure they will be able to move themselves around if they roll over in their sleep. If their arms are still swaddled down at this age and they roll over, it could create an incredibly dangerous situation.

For many babies, swaddling helps them feel comforted and secure. Even if some babies resist being swaddled at first, it is best to keep trying to swaddle your baby as it often takes time to get used to swaddle. Swaddling has been known to increase sleep efficiency while keeping your baby cozy. The swaddle replicates a womb-like feel for your baby and they might find peace with the swaddle. Swaddling can also help to eliminate or decrease the Moro reflex. This reflex is a response to stimulation felt by your baby and typically will go away between three to six months of age. The Moro reflex is a startle reflex that can often wake your baby from a deep sleep. Their arms will likely flair out and shake a bit before fluttering or opening their eyes. The Moro reflex is very normal with newborn babies but can greatly impact sleep for your child. When you swaddle your baby, you will swaddle your baby's arms down tightly and they will be unable to startle easily throughout the night. In turn, eliminating the startle reflex will ensure this isn't the cause of your baby waking up so frequently throughout the night. Many babies like being swaddled and look to their swaddle for extra comfort and relaxation. Your baby spent nine months swaddled and cozy so it would make sense that it would enjoy feeling that sensation again.

Wearable blankets are incredibly popular as they provide your child with the warmth they need safely. Since the blanket is worn and often zipped up and around your baby, the likelihood of this type of blanket being hazardous is incredibly minimal. Wearable blankets can vary in material and warmth and can be changed along with the seasons and as your baby grows. When your child can walk, many wearable blankets have holes for their feet so they can freely move around in the crib while staying warm. Using a wearable blanket will also prevent your child from throwing the blanket off and can be used as a sleep cue for your child. Many children know that when they put their wearable blanket on, that sleep is near. You will find that these blankets come in different shapes, sizes, materials and some even replicate a hand on your baby's chest with lightly weighted material. Many babies rely on their parent's touch to comfort them and put them back to sleep. Many wearable blankets have replicated this feeling for babies and can be considered during sleep training if you feel they will benefit from this type of blanket.

Sleep props or sleep cues are incredibly important to signal to your baby that it's time to sleep. Throughout your established nighttime routine, you will need to include items that signal to your child that it's time to sleep. Items like a wearable blanket, books, and a lovey are good options to include in the routine. A lovey is a small stuffed animal that is safe and approved for sleep. Often, children like to hold onto something at night or have something close by. Please do not confuse this with a regular stuffed animal thrown in your child's crib. A lovey is a safe sleep prop that will be free of suffocation or choking hazards and should only be used when your child is ready for one. Newborns for example who are swaddled will not have any use for a lovey and cannot make the connection between the lovey and sleep. You can try introducing different loveys to your child to see if they gravitate to any one of them. If your child is going to have a lovey, they will most likely show you that they are interested when you give it to them. It might take some time for them to get used to the lovey when it sleeps. Keep in mind that when a child attaches to a lovey, you need to make sure that it's ready and available for all naps and night sleep so that your baby knows that the lovey is part of its routine. The lovey can also keep the baby company, so it doesn't feel as though it is alone in its crib each night. It'll have a friend with it to sleep with and cuddle. Loveys are often held by mom for some time to get mother's scent on the lovey. When the child then sleeps with the lovey, it is comforted by mom's scent on the lovey and feels as though their mother is close by. This can also be done with your child's sheets. Be sure to try different options when working to identify the best sleep props for your baby.

If your baby uses a binky, this can also be used as a sleep prop. We'll get into how to use the binky during sleep training in chapter eight but for now, you must decide whether or not a binky is right for your baby. If your baby is already using one, it will be most effective during the program, if it is not, you can try introducing a binky to your baby but you might find that it rejects it. Be prepared for both circumstances to occur. Binkies are a great way to quiet and calm your baby when it is upset. Many babies normally use one while they sleep because it mimics sucking and this is also very soothing.

A sound machine is another critical and very effective sleep prop for your baby. Turning a sound machine on at night and for naps is a great sleep cue for your baby. It is also a nice addition to any nighttime routine that you might be following. When a baby hears their sound machine go on, they will know that sleep time is quickly approaching. Sound machines often replicate the sounds babies hear in the womb and provide peaceful sounds for your baby. Sound machines also drowned out outside noise that might wake your baby. Specifically, if you have multiple family members living in your home, you will not be able to always keep your home completely silent for your baby. When you use a sound machine, most outside noises will not be heard by your baby and they will be more likely to stay in a deep sleep. The sound machine will also work as a sleep cue for your baby. Turning the machine on right before your baby goes to sleep, will mean they begin to connect the sound machine with going to sleep. When it hears the sounds, it will know and be more aware that sleep is coming soon. Research shows that sound machines not only help your baby to fall asleep more quickly and peacefully, but it helps them move into a deeper sleep. When your baby is at peace, it will be able to sleep better. Listening to soothing sounds at night will help them achieve sleep success at night and during the day at nap time. Most machines are equipped with different sounds that range from ocean waves, rain, and heartbeats. Find what works best for your baby. You might need to try out each sound before you rely on one to ensure it's the best fit. Be sure not to exceed the maximum volume of the sound machine as your baby's ears are incredibly sensitive. You will also need to place the sound machine at least seven feet away from your baby. Placing the machine too close to your baby is not safe for your baby's hearing.

A rocking chair is a nice addition to any nursery or room where your baby will be sleeping. Rocking chairs and gliders are not only comfortable for you, but they are incredibly soothing for your baby. Babies are used to constant movements from living in the womb and find this type of rocking very peaceful. You will find that you will likely get an immense amount of use out of a glider or rocking chair if you choose to bring one into your home. Gliders for example are great because they allow you to pick your feet up while you're rocking your baby. When you're tired and exhausted from a long day and you just want your baby to relax, rocking them in a glider with your feet up is a great way to wind down from the day with your baby. Rocking your baby during their nighttime routine is also beneficial. They will be soothed and ready for sleep once they're done rocking. Most parents enjoy nursing or bottle-feeding their baby while they rock in a chair. As time goes on, the rocking chair will be a place where you can cuddle with your baby, read, tell stories, and just relax. Be sure to invest in a good quality chair that will last for many years to come. You will get your use out of it with all the rocking you will be doing over the coming months and years. Now that you have your rocking chair, it's time to discuss what to avoid with the chair. You do not want the chair to be a sleep crutch for your baby. One that it needs to fall asleep at night. Parents often rock their baby at night or before naps until they are completely asleep. When this happens, babies do not self soothe, and they are unable to put themselves to sleep on their own. Relying on rocking for your baby to fall asleep can create unhealthy sleep habits and it will be more difficult to get your baby to sleep on their own when the time comes. That's not to say that you can't rock your baby at night. You absolutely can and should rock them each night. What this is saying is that you must avoid rocking them until they completely fall asleep. When it is rocked to sleep and you try to put it down in its crib or bassinet at night, you will likely find that it wakes up and begins to cry for you to pick it up again. Babies will get used to sleeping in our arms if we consistently let them over time and it will be difficult to stop this from happening the longer we allow it to happen. Be sure that you use your rocker to simply rock your baby for comfort instead of rocking them until they are completely asleep. This can also be done with yoga balls. Yoga balls are becoming increasingly popular when it comes to putting a baby down to sleep at night. Yoga balls are big enough and sturdy enough for a parent to bounce on while holding their baby at night. Using a yoga ball can be a great addition to any bedtime routine but should not be used as a crutch or a way to get your baby to sleep each night. A yoga ball is very similar to a rocker in that a baby will get used to bouncing and will then rely on bouncing to fall asleep each time. If you choose to use a yoga ball, be sure that you are mindful of the amount of time spent on the ball each day when putting your baby down for a nap or during their nightly routine.

Chapter 6.
Establish a Consistent Routine

Establishing a clear and consistent nighttime routine is critical for sleep success. Following your routine and doing the same things in the same order will ensure that your child begins to understand that bedtime is imminent. Beginning a routine as early as six to eight weeks will ensure that your baby will begin to understand what to expect at night. If your child is beyond this age, have no fear, beginning a routine at any age will be successful as long as you truly take the time to commit what it takes to make it stick. The routine can be completely customized and easy to follow. You will want to stay as close to the routine each night as possible for your baby to get comfortable with the routine. The more the routine occurs, the more likely it will be that your baby will begin to expect what comes next in the routine. They will be more aware of the fact that it's getting close to the time they sleep, and they will be able to mentally prepare. Babies, like adults, like to know what to expect and what's coming next. If you try and put your baby down without following a routine, this could be very traumatic for them. The key is to ease your child into sleep mode so that by the time it lays down, it is ready to rest for the night. If this is done too early or without winding down, it might cause the situation to escalate and your baby might get upset. When you ease your child into sleeping for the night, you're more likely to find that it falls asleep much easier and without hesitation. Think about it this way, are you able to fall asleep immediately after talking with friends or being in a loud, bright space? Most likely, this is not the case. It will take you some time to wind down, relax, and get ready for sleep. Regardless of what your routine looks like, remaining consistent with your routine is critical for success. If you are constantly changing or not following your routine, it will be difficult for your baby to become familiar with the routine. Consistency is key. You will need to repeat the same routine over many nights before your child knows what to expect. Be sure that you remain consistent and keep your routine the same each night if you can. The routine should be done by both parents that way your child is familiar with following the routine with both of you. You don't want only one person to be the only one who can put your child to sleep at night. Be sure that your child is familiar with following this routine with both of you as life happens and you will not always be able to be the only person putting your child to sleep at night. There will likely come a time when you need to switch and let someone else follow the routine with your baby.

Before you establish a routine, you will need to first identify a bedtime for your baby. For most babies, the sweet spot for night sleep is somewhere between 6:30 and 8:00 PM. Be sure not to put your baby to bed after 8:00 PM. This is critical to avoid the second wind. Once a baby has missed their initial tired phase, they move into the second wind and it will be incredibly difficult to get them back to sleep. After 8:00 PM babies get a surge of energy that will be difficult to bring down if you miss putting your baby down during the identified time of 7:00 PM-8:00 PM. Once you choose a time that works for your baby, try to stay consistent each night and put them down at the same time. After a few nights of your routine and your designated bedtime, your baby will begin to get very sleep as it gets closer to its bedtime. When this happens, it will be much easier to put your baby down at this time because its body is already familiar with sleeping at this time. Staying consistent with your bedtime is very important. That's not to say there won't be nights when you get home late or get your baby to bed later than expected but for most nights, you want to remain as consistent as possible. During the two weeks of sleep training, you will need to keep your baby's bedtime the same each night to ensure the program is the most effective. Parents often think that if they put their baby down later at night that they will sleep in, in the morning. That would mean that parents would be able to sleep in a bit too. Unfortunately, that's simply not the case. Another common myth is that avoiding naps during the day will also help your baby sleep better at night when in fact, this is just the opposite. Making sure your baby has enough naps during the day, according to their age and needs will allow them to sleep much better at night. Sticking to the identified sleep time at night and during the day is the best for your baby as this is when they are the most tired and willing to sleep. If you push too far beyond their bedtime, you may find that they are now overly tired, irritable, and unable to sleep. Waiting too long to put your baby to sleep at night can also lead to frequent night waking and also waking up very early. Babies who are put down to sleep between 6:30-8:00 PM are known to sleep better and for longer periods. Before identifying a bedtime, you will also need to take into consideration when their second nap of the day was and how long it lasted. For babies to sleep their best, their bedtime should be at least two to three hours after their last nap. For example, if their last nap ended at 3:30 PM, a good time for their bedtime would be 6:30 PM. Babies will need enough time to get tired again before they go to sleep at night. If you try to put your baby down before it is tired and ready to sleep, this will also cause irritability and you might find yourself struggling and frustrated. Be sure that you are aware of their last nap to appropriately choose a bedtime. Keeping your baby's naptime and nighttime sleep at consistent times each day will ensure that your baby will start becoming familiar with the time it needs to sleep and it will also begin preparing itself for its naps and to be put down for bed at night. The goal is to get your baby on a night and day routine so that their body is ready for sleep at designated times throughout the day and night which will make it much easier for you to get them down for their naps and the night. Be patient and know that within time, your baby's internal clock will begin to kick in and they will know when it is time to sleep. Remember, during months one and two your baby is unable to even decipher between night and day. Give them some time to understand that sleep happens at different times of the day and night. Each baby will be different but with consistency, the routine will begin to stick for your baby.

The routine can be as basic as you would like it to be. It doesn't have to be complicated or full of steps, it just needs to be calming and phase into sleep. For example, a typical nighttime routine for a baby might begin with a warm bath, followed by a baby massage, putting pajamas and wearable blanket on, bedtime story, nurse/rock for ten minutes, and then lay baby down. Remember, the routine can be customized to your liking and preferences. Including a warm bath before bed is very common because it relaxes the baby. If you choose to include a warm bath before bed, you might want to use calming bath bubbles that include lavender and chamomile. Both lavender and chamomile are known to produce a calming feel for babies and the smell is incredibly soothing. There are organic bath bubbles for sensitive skin that can be used as well. You might choose to dim the lights when you're bathing your baby. Be sure the light isn't too dim as you will need to be able to effectively see your baby while bathing them. If you choose to keep the lights dim, be sure that you continue keeping the lights dim after the bath. If you move the baby into a well-lit room after the bath, it might move the baby into a more of an awake mode. Keeping the lights dim in your baby's room will help keep the baby in a soothing and relaxing mode after its bath.

After you've given your baby a warm bath, you will want to follow the rest of the night routine in their room. This is done so that the baby gets used to being in its room and it will begin to feel much more comfortable for it. If you're constantly switching rooms, this might confuse your baby. For example, if you get your baby dressed in the living room where it normally plays, it might get confused and think that it's time to play. Moving them into the nursery for the night routine will encourage them to start associating its room with sleep. Now that you're in the room where your baby sleeps, it might be helpful to play soft and soothing music during your routine. Meditation music and soothing sounds are very helpful in relaxing your baby. Be sure not to turn the volume up too high if you choose to utilize meditation music or other relaxing sounds. Before you get your baby dressed for the night, consider giving your baby a massage. Baby massages are becoming increasingly popular before bed as they help relax the baby's muscles and help move them into a relaxing state. The baby massage can be done with or without lotion. If you choose to use lotion, be sure the lotion is unscented as strong scents can be disturbing for babies and this scent might distract them from falling asleep. That being said, scents like lavender and chamomile are fine to use and are recommended due to their calming effects. This type of massage therapy for babies can help them get to sleep better, it can help improve their health and circulation and it can even help you develop a stronger bond with your baby. Research shows that giving your baby a massage can also help reduce fussiness and crying. Other ailments like constipation and colic might also be alleviated or eliminated by giving your baby a massage. Constipation and colic have been known to interfere with baby's sleep. Knowing that baby massages might help this will give you another tool to help your child sleep well by eliminating factors that might impact their sleep efficiency. While giving your baby a massage, you will be showing them, love, while improving their digestion, muscle development all while encouraging healthy sleep for your baby.

Now that you've identified a consistent routine for your baby and an appropriate bedtime, you will need to address nursing and feedings. If you're nursing your baby, this will likely be a part of your bedtime routine. For many mothers who choose to nurse, they will nurse their baby before going to bed at night. This will ensure that your baby stays full throughout the night, it will calm your baby and help them prepare for sleep and it will also ensure that you keep your milk supply. With that said, nursing can also be a sleep crutch for babies, and they might want to nurse consistently until they fall asleep. The problem with this is that once they fall asleep, they are now attached to you and it will be incredibly difficult to put your baby down and into their crib. What can often happen is the baby will nurse, fall asleep and then once you go to put your baby down, it will wake up, begin to cry and you will have to start the routine all over again. This can be a vicious cycle. If you're nursing and able, you will want to nurse your baby at bedtime. This will create a calming and soothing atmosphere for your baby. Your baby will feel close and comforted by you and nursing will make it sleepy. Nursing your baby has been known to make mother and baby sleepy due to the release of a gastrointestinal hormone, cholecystokinin. That being said, you will not want to nurse your baby right before laying them down at night because they will begin to need to nurse to fall asleep. They will start to rely on nursing to soothe themselves and in turn, will not be able to fall asleep on their own. If you have already been doing this, that's ok. During the sleep training program, you will identify steps that you can take to change this. You will also not want to nurse your baby too close to laying them down to avoid any potential spit-ups from occurring. If your baby cries during the sleep training program, you will want to make sure those tears do not cause them to spit up their milk from being overly agitated. To try and avoid this, be sure to nurse your baby at least thirty minutes before you put them down in their crib. If it's too hard for you to be this close to your baby without nursing them because it is too distracted by your milk, you might need to have your partner finish off the nighttime routine with your baby. Remember that babies can smell your milk, and this can not only be a distraction for them, but they will also likely want to keep nursing even after they're full just for the ongoing comfort they feel when they nurse.

Chapter 7.
Self- Soothing: Letting your baby put themselves to sleep

It's important to get your baby ready for bed in their own room because we want them to feel safe and secure in their room. We want this to be a place of comfort for them where they know they receive lots of love, hugs and kisses from their parents. This is important because we want to be sure your baby feels your love and comfort before bed. This will instill trust and they will know that when you put them down alone in their crib that they are safe and can fall asleep. We want to be sure that they know their crib is a safe and peaceful place. If your baby feels stressed, overwhelmed or doesn't feel a sense of love or comfort coming from you during the nightly routine, it might feel as though something is off. It might begin to feel anxious and in turn, might resist moving into its crib altogether. The ultimate goal of following a sleep training program is getting your baby to a place where it can fully put itself to sleep. When your baby can fall asleep on their own, it means that they have successfully mastered the skill of soothing themselves. Self-soothing is critical for sleep success. Most babies do not have this skill mastered and following a sleep training program will put them in a position where they will gradually learn and master this skill over time.

Minimize rocking, nursing, and bouncing to sleep. It is your baby's job to get themselves to sleep each night, not yours. Parents often think that we must get our baby to a place when they are completely asleep before we can try to remove ourselves from the room. It is your job as a parent to help your baby unwind and relax for the day. It is not your job to get them drowsy. They will begin to learn this skill on their own and on time. We, as parents are there to give them the tools to do so until they are fully able to figure this process out on their own. If your baby starts to drift off while you are nursing or bottle-feeding, sit them up so that it wakes. This is of vital importance as you do not want them to fall asleep when they are eating. This might require you to turn the lights on in the room if they are having trouble staying awake. You might even need to nurse them before you put on their pajamas and sleep sack or wearable blanket to be sure that they do not fall asleep. Your baby can close their eyes during their night feeding but be sure that they do not drift off. This is likely to happen quite often before you put your baby down but taking steps to avoid this will ensure that it does not relate nursing or eating to falling asleep and will not rely on this. One strategy that you can use to ensure this doesn't happen is to keep track of how long you are nursing your baby. If you typically nurse your baby for twenty to thirty minutes each night and they fall asleep after this amount of time, you will want to shorten the amount of time you nurse. If you're not sure how long you typically nurse, have your partner time the minutes and then log this information. Doing so will help you prepare and will keep you prepared for sleep training. You will want to track and identify the amount of time before you begin the program, so you know where to start. If you are following the steps provided on how to prepare for sleep training, you will know that your baby will have received enough calories and nutrients during the day with his feedings that you've increased. As discussed, by increasing the number of feedings your baby receives during the day, you will be assured that it will need much less at night. This should give you the peace of mind that you will likely need when it comes time to remove your baby and stop nursing them. Many mothers tend to worry that your baby is still hungry and needs to keep nursing when in fact they are more often than not, nursing for comfort and not for the nutrients at this point.

Depending on the age of your baby, it might require an extra feeding at night. You also might want to include a dream feed into your nightly routine if you feel that your baby is constantly waking up hungry each night. This night feeding will help them sleep the rest of the night with a full tummy. Babies who typically go to bed between 6:00 PM-8:00 PM can genuinely be hungry at night and need extra calories to get the sleep they need. One strategy that is often used is the dream feed. Specifically, while you are following a sleep training program, you will learn that dream feeding your baby can not only be incredibly effective but will help them sleep much longer throughout the night without waking. The dream feed is essentially what you will do to "top off" your baby and keep them full without actually waking him. You will be gently moving your baby without fully waking them. You can either identify a certain time of the night to do this or you can dream feed your baby around the same time you are ready to go to bed. If you put your baby to bed at 7:00 PM, a good time to go in for a dream feed is around 10:00 PM or 11:00 PM. By this time, around five or so hours have passed since your baby's last feeding. Feeding them at this time will help ensure that it stays asleep for at least another five to seven hours. It's worth noting that for babies who frequently wake during the night to nurse or feed, including two dream feeding sessions into the nightly routine might be effective, especially as you move through the sleep training program. The point of dream feeding is to address the issue before your baby wakes up on its own and begins to cry. If it wakes up at certain times of the night to feed, try dream feeding him at least thirty minutes before it normally wakes up to nurse. For example, if your baby typically wakes around 11:00 PM and 3:30 AM to nurse, it's best if you dream feed your baby at 10:30PM and 3:00 AM to get to them before it has the chance to wake up and cry. You might need to set an alarm to be sure that you wake up in time to feed them. This can be difficult but will be worth it once your baby can sleep on its own. Dream feedings will not last forever and typically will only occur for a few months. Waking up to dream feed your baby is much easier than waking up to baby cries and then trying to get them back to sleep after that. At that point, it becomes even harder to get your baby back to sleep. Addressing this before it has a chance to wake and cry will keep them sleeping throughout the night without waking.

Dream feeds are great for any baby as they will get extra calories they need to sleep better, and the meal is not in a response to them crying. They will also begin to eat less and less at night with dream feeds which will, in turn, boost their hunger in the morning. When it is hungrier in the morning, it will be more likely to consume more calories and feed more during the day. To appropriately dream feed your baby, you will need to follow these steps. First, you will move quietly into your baby's room. Be careful not to turn a light on or make loud noises. For this reason, it might be helpful to have a nightlight in your baby's room to avoid any falls or loud movements. Once you're close to the crib, you will gently take your baby out of the crib. Make sure that you take your baby out and do not try to lean over and into the crib to nurse or bottle-feed as this could not only be frustrating but also hard on your back and not the most effective way to dream feed your baby. Once you're gently holding your baby, place the bottle or your breast if you're nursing on your baby's lip to see if it starts feeding. Remember, it will not be fully awake at this time. Try to get your baby to feed for at least five to ten minutes but no longer than that timeframe. Remember, you are just "toping him off." Be sure to offer both sides if you're nursing to keep up your milk supply. This can also be very painful if you haven't expressed milk from both breasts at the same time. This will not be a full feeding and you do not want to risk waking them up during this time. This is going to be a quick process where you move in and out without them even realizing that you were there. If it wakes and realizes that you're holding them, it will likely be incredibly difficult for you to get them back down to sleep. After you dream feed your baby, you will also want to burp them. Always burp your baby after a feeding. If you do not burp them, this could cause them to spit up or develop a reflux condition. Gently put your baby on your shoulder and ever so gently pat their back until it burps. Lay your baby back down and quietly exit the room. Follow this dream feed routine until your baby has been sleeping successfully for at least four weeks. In time, and with the sleep training program, you will find that you will no longer need to dream feed your baby and will then be able to remove this from your nightly routine. If you find that your baby is unable to fall asleep after a dream feed, you might need to remove the dream feed from your nightly routine. For some babies, the dream feed interrupts their deep sleep and they find it difficult to get back to sleep after their parent has woken them. If you find that this is the situation for your baby, and it has happened multiple times, dream feeding might not be the best solution.

Chapter 8.
Week 1 of Sleep Training

At this point, you are as prepared as possible and it's time to begin the first week of sleep training. You've followed all of the steps, created a solid routine and healthy sleep atmosphere for your baby and mentally prepared for this program. Now it's time to begin and put everything that you've learned into action. As you move throughout the program, and you hit roadblocks, different moments and start to potentially question why you started in the first place, remind yourself of the goal and know that it will take your baby at least three days to become familiar with this new routine. Do not give up after the first night because it's difficult. Try your very best to remain diligent and clear with your goal and expectations. On day one of the program, be sure to wake your baby up at a designated time. We want them to start getting familiar with waking up at the same time each day. This will allow them to adjust to naps at specific times each day and will also ensure that it is ready for bed at the bedtime of choice. Keep in mind, this will take a few days for them to get used to. Just like adults, babies need time to adjust to waking and going to sleep at designated times of the day. To the best of our ability, we want to create a predictable daily schedule for your baby. This will make your days and nights much easier when you know the exact time to put your baby down for their naps and bedtime. With that said, working with a baby can sometimes be unpredictable. The goal here is to adjust right alongside your baby while doing your best to implement a strategic plan to follow each day.

When you wake your baby up for the day, be sure to open the blinds, turn lights on, and make sure the room is bright. We want to be sure that your baby connects the light to being awake and daytime. If the room is kept dark, they might get confused and want to fall back asleep. During sleep training and beyond, we want to be sure your baby differentiates between night and day. Babies will be able to reorganize their circadian rhythm with natural light. Part of this process ensures that when a baby wakes up and it's light outside, they know that this is the time to get up for the day. When they wake up at night or very early morning and it's still dark, they will start to understand that darkness is meant for sleeping and will then put themselves back to sleep instead of crying and requesting that you come in and pick them up. They will automatically know that it's time to keep sleeping. When it's morning and your baby is up and ready for the day, be sure to change your baby out of their pajamas and get them dressed in daytime clothes. We want to be sure that we're following a routine during the day just as we follow a routine at night. This will get the baby used to certain actions that take place during the day and those that occur at night. Doing this consistently will familiarize your baby with your expectations and the actions that should be taking place at different times. They will then be more prepared for different actions to occur. When a baby is prepared and understands what comes next, they are less likely to feel anxious, cry, or want to be held. Just like adults, the more prepared we are, the better we feel and the more positive our outlook will be on what's ahead and approaching.

Now that your baby is up for the day, is dressed in daytime clothes and the room and house is bright, you want to encourage a great deal of playtime with your baby. Create a bright space where your baby can play with toys, read books, roll around, and stay active. This is the time when you can tickle your baby's feet, dance, sing to more upbeat music, take walks outside and show your baby that this is the time to be alert, stay awake and use your energy. We are working to differentiate day and night actions while also ensuring that your baby uses all of its energy during the day so when night comes, it is tired from the day and ready for bed. If your baby hasn't used its energy during the day, you've kept the light off or dim outside of nap times and didn't have enough time to play, it will be much more difficult for them to go to sleep. This will be challenging for you because, at this point, it will be too late for you to take them outside or get them to play to the extent that they should have played during the day. Setting up a consistent playtime schedule will not only help your baby sleep, but it will also support them developmentally and physically. The more active we are, the more we move our muscles during the day, the more likely we are to be exhausted at night and ready for bed. During this program, we are consistently working on the actions that take place at night, but we are also working on those that occur during the day. This will create a consistent and well-rounded schedule. We want your baby to perceive the differences that take place at different times.

Now, we are ready to begin. You've got this! During weeks one and two, you will follow the bedtime routine and get your baby ready for bed. Remember, nurse or bottle-feed your baby thirty minutes before you lay them down. This is vital because if it begins to cry, it will be less likely to spit up and require your attention. When it's time to lay your baby down, tell them how much you love them and that you are there for them. Make sure it hears your voice and feels your comfort before laying it down in its crib. Reassure it that you will be by its side throughout this process. This is helpful for your baby to hear and it will bring you some peace as well. Once you lay them down, be sure that you leave the room. When you lay them down, be sure that it is still awake. This is the single, most important thing that you must do. For it to learn how to sleep on its own, you absolutely must lay them down in their crib each night while they are still awake. They can and should be drowsy, but still very much awake. Some parents choose to stay in the room while their baby falls asleep to make sure their baby knows they are there for them. For most babies, it's much harder to fall asleep if they know their parents are close for that reason, it's recommended that you completely remove yourself from the room once you lay them down. During this time, your baby might begin to cry and fuss. Do not go back in and pick them up. Baby cries can be very difficult and agonizing for parents to hear. We all feel this way. We never want to hear our baby scream and cry especially if we know that there is something we can do that will make it stop. When this happens, you must continue reminding yourself of the result. The goal of this part of the training is to teach your child that crying at night will not get a reaction from you unless genuinely needed. Babies, like adults, understand cause and effect. They understand that when they do something, it causes a reaction and continue this action to get the same response. On night three, four and beyond, you will only use your voice to reassure them that you're there. You will not be laying them down or touching them.

While sleep training, we want to teach our baby that crying at night will not get our attention, but we will be there, helping and supporting without a response. We will do everything we can to stay as calm as possible. If you find yourself struggling throughout the process go back to your journal and read what you wrote about why you started sleep training. Try imagining yourself waking up refreshed and able to be a better parent now that you're getting the sleep you need. Think about your baby being less cranky and getting solid, impactful sleep each night. Remember, you are there for your baby throughout the entire process, but you need to teach your baby that it can put itself to sleep without the help of its parents. This is the time to watch your baby on the monitor to track their movements. For most parents, this is the most difficult part of sleep training, hearing your baby cry and not being able to go in their room and do anything about it. This is pulling on your heartstrings and you will most likely feel every urge and impulse to want to go in and pick your baby up. For the sake of getting your child the sleep it needs, you must do everything you possibly can to avoid going into their room. This is when you will need to follow the steps listed and find a way to distract yourself while still paying attention to the time and the baby monitor. Remember, it will be worth it all at the end of the training and you will be glad that you followed these steps. Your baby will likely scream and yell from time to time and you must stay strong. Leaving your baby in their crib at this time does not mean that you're a bad parent. It means that you're an amazing parent that wants to ensure that your baby gets the sleep that it needs. Babies communicate through crying and their cries do not always mean that they are in pain or desperately need something. It just means that they are thinking and saying, "What's going on here? Why has the situation changed?" Throughout the time your baby is crying, we will be monitoring the time and the length of time they are crying, and we will also be on the lookout for sleep-promoting behaviors. During this time, we will use the monitor to see if your baby is beginning to do things that will soothe them to sleep. We will be looking for behaviors that include; mumbling and talking to themselves, sucking on their hand, and moving their head from side to side. These are all actions that will lead them to sleep. Even if it is crying while it is showing these behaviors, this is a very good sign. If it doesn't do this on night one, that's ok too. These behaviors will come in time and will show us that it is on its way to successful sleep.

On night one, you will be able to "pop-in" once it has been crying for some time. The pop-in schedule will look like this:

Five minutes of crying- pop in

Ten minutes of crying- pop in

Fifteen minutes of crying- pop in

After each pop in, begin timing to be sure you stick to this schedule until your baby falls asleep. After each pop in, the time between will increase by five minutes, ten minutes, and so on. The goal here is to get your baby used to going longer and longer periods without having you come in until it finally reaches a point when it completely falls asleep. During this time, you might find that your baby adheres to the rollercoaster method of crying. The roller coaster method shows a baby crying increases over time, gets to a point when crying is at its strongest before dropping down and decreasing once it has hit its peak of crying. Your baby is trying to get your attention during this time and feels that if it cries louder and stronger, you will come in. We don't want to reward this behavior by pop-ins but we do want to strategically time the pop-ins to ensure they are impactful. Many sleep training programs do not allow for pop-ins to take place and require you to leave your baby alone and not come back once you lay them down. This can be incredibly difficult for both baby and mom and dad. The method you will find here allows you to be there for your baby while letting them find their way. This is the goal. At the end of sleep training, your baby should be able to put itself right back to sleep each time it wakes during the night.

During pop-ins if you find that your baby gets particularly upset, it might be helpful to have your partner do the pop-ins. Pay attention to the reaction of your baby. If you find that it responds differently to one of you over the other, it's probably best to have the parent who it gives the more positive reaction to do the pop-ins. We want to avoid having your baby get even more upset. When you are popping in, you are not staying long, and you are not picking your baby up. Each pop in should only last for fifteen to twenty seconds and no longer than that. What you can do is rest your hand on your baby, rub its head, and tell it that you're there and that you love it. We want your baby to know that you are with them throughout this process and you will be with them every step of the way. You can also lay your baby back down if it is standing or sitting up but only once during each pop in. Once this is done you will exit the room and continue watching the monitor. If it is still crying during the second pop in, try increasing the volume of the sound machine, be sure its binky is in its mouth, and gently pat your baby for a few seconds before removing yourself again. Check the sound machine to be sure it will stay on all night. If the sound machine shuts off in the middle of the night, it might wake your baby from a deep sleep. Continue to repeat this process each time you go in to check on your baby. Remember, your baby can sense your stress levels so try to remain as calm as possible while reassuring your baby each time you pop in to see it. This is easier said than done but if you can be mindful about your emotions and what you're expressing and feeling, this will not only be helpful for you but also your baby. If at any time you feel that pop-ins are causing your baby to become even more upset, you can eliminate them and simply continue watching the monitor to ensure that your baby has all that it needs to get itself to sleep. You can always customize the plan along the way. Don't be afraid to do what makes sense for you as long as you keep the main goal in mind. If you choose to customize along the way, just be sure to keep the critical components of the program in mind.

An example of what your efforts might look like during night one and two:

First pop in: Gently pat your baby, rub their head and hair. Lay them down if they are sitting or standing. Tell them you love them and you're there for them.

Watch and wait

Second pop in: Repeat the same process as above. Gradually increase the sound machine

Watch and wait

Third pop in: Repeat steps.

Continue pop-ins until your baby falls asleep

As you move through the night, you will want to keep the designated time between each pop in, in mind. You will be popping in after five minutes, ten minutes, and fifteen minutes. The same rules apply to pop-ins in the middle of the night. Remember, you will not be picking your baby up as this will be confusing for them. You must avoid confusing your baby at all costs. Confusing them will prevent them from progressing throughout the plan. They will not understand what you're asking of them if you are picking them up at times and other times you leave them to cry in their crib. You will however be soothing them by rubbing their head, telling them you love them, and laying them back down in their crib if they are standing or sitting up. It will be helpful to journal or chart each time you pop into their room at night so you can look back at your progress. Remember to start with the same duration between pop-ins during each night waking. Every time your baby wakes up at night, you will start the process over again starting with popping in after five minutes, ten, and so on. Night pop-ins are tough. You're exhausted and want to move back to the easier solution and do whatever it takes just to get them back to sleep. Night waking causes many parents to forget all the work they've done and revert to old habits. Stay strong and consistent during night waking. Keep a goal sheet next to your bed at night or encourage your partner to remind you of why you both started this program. It will be tough, but you can do it. Work with your baby to identify what it needs. In time, you will identify what works best for your family. For example, if your baby gets even more upset after the third pop in, you might want to remove this from the routine as long as you're confident their safe. In time, you will see your baby spend less and less time putting itself back to sleep at night and you will greatly benefit from the progress it is making.

If your baby wakes at any point during the goal wake time of approximately 6:15 AM to 7:15 AM with a bedtime of around 7:15 PM, go right to them and pick them up even if they are crying. If your baby wakes up before 6:30 AM, it will need to be left in its crib until the normal time that you take them out, approximately 7:00 AM. We want to assure them that they done all the right things by waking up at the time that they are supposed to. If your baby wakes up before the designated time, pretend that it is still the middle of the night and prepare to do pop-ins just as you would any other time. Even if it's only one hour before the designated time for your baby to wake up. You will continue to do pop-ins until the designated time is reached and then you can pick up your baby but only when they are quiet. Notice the difference here. If your baby wakes up when she is supposed to and they are crying, you may pick them up. If your baby is crying after you've done pop-ins and have now reached the designated wake up time, wait until they are quiet before you pick them up. We want to reinforce the quiet moments, not the moments when they are crying. When your baby is awake, give them snuggles and kisses and tell them that they did a wonderful job. We want to encourage them by giving them lots of praise and compliments. Be sure to turn lights on and make the room nice and bright now that they are awake. We want to be sure they know that the time has changed and now it's daytime. You will also want to feed them in the living room or somewhere other than their room. We do not want to confuse them and have them continue thinking that this is an extension of their night sleep.

Avoid staying glued to the monitor. Parents often stay up all night staring at their baby on the monitor. This isn't healthy either and you won't be allowing yourself to sleep and rest when you should be. Being overly concerned with every move your baby makes while it is in its crib and not by your side can be unhealthy. Be sure to pay attention to the monitor without feeling overly connected to it. Once your baby falls asleep, be prepared for them to wake throughout the night. Be sure to include a dream feed if this is appropriate for your baby. Remember including a dream feed into your nightly routine will help prevent your baby from waking throughout the night. They may still wake but the dream feed is an extra step that you can take to prevent this from happening. If your baby wakes up throughout the night and you've included the dream feed, you will need to restart the watch and wait process. This will involve paying attention to the baby monitor to identify whether or not your baby truly needs your support. If it doesn't, which it most likely will not, begin watching and waiting before doing any pop-ins. Remember, you never have to do a pop in. If you find that it's too difficult in the middle of the night and your baby becomes too upset or it's difficult for you not to pick them up, feel free to remove this from the program. If you feel that your baby is fine and you are confident, a pop-in isn't necessary. The most critical time for pop-ins is at the start of the night. We want to be sure they are reassured that you are there and close by if it truly needs you. This is when it is learning that it is not being left alone. You can also spread out the time between pop-ins if you find that to be more helpful for your baby.

Week 2 of Sleep Training

Week one is done. You have accomplished the hardest part of the program. At this point in the program, you want to make sure that you remain consistent. Now is the time when many parents fall back into old habits. They move back into the room where their child is sleeping. They push bedtime back due to other engagements. This is the time that it becomes difficult to keep moving and stay consistent in the second week. If you found success in week one, you might be thinking that your baby doesn't need to follow the program anymore and that it has accomplished sleep training! But wait a minute, yes, your baby is on track for success. They are doing well, has been sleeping much better. When you first started the program, it took your baby almost forty minutes to fall asleep. Now, after week one, they are falling asleep in twenty minutes. That's a huge success! You should feel incredibly proud of your baby, yourself, and all that you've accomplished together. That being said, we still have more work to do. Do not quit now just because you've found success in the program. We want to ensure that the skills learned by your baby this week stick. We want to make sure it doesn't quickly revert to its old sleeping habits and we want to make sure that you, as their parent also stay consistent with developing healthy sleep habits. Developing healthy sleep habits take more than a week. You must remember that when you are working through this program. The program is scheduled for two weeks but in reality, it will take you much longer to fully instill healthy sleep habits into your baby. You will find success after two weeks, but you will have to keep at it to be sure the program is most effective. The best thing that you can do during this time is to stay consistent. Let your baby know that it is doing a great job. Celebrate the week of wins and prepare for week two. This might seem like a long process but in the end, it will all be worth it. Dedicating two weeks will lead you to many months and years of sleep success with your baby and toddler.

Over the next few days, you will work to decrease the number of night feedings offered. When it comes to the dream feed, we will slowly shorten the amount of time we feed the baby at night until eventually, we can drop the dream feeds altogether. After night one, you will be slightly decreasing your baby's consumption. Most parents choose to begin night weening in week two, but this can be done in week one if you wish just as long as you have accomplished night one of sleep training. You might choose to alter this program to extend it or shorten it if you find that your baby no longer needs night feedings sooner than seven days after beginning. This process is geared toward mothers who are nursing and have typically nursed their baby multiple times at night to get them back to sleep. You will first need to know how long you nurse your baby during one or both night feedings. From there, you will decrease the amount you nurse by five and then three minutes during each feeding. Feel free to create your schedule but a sample schedule might look like this:

Night 1 Continue to nurse/feed as you normally would

Night 2 of Night Weening

11:00 PM 20 Minutes

4:00 AM 20 Minutes

Night 3 of Night Weening

11:00PM 15 Minutes

4:00AM 15 Minutes

Night 4 of Night Weening

11:00PM 12 Minutes

4:00AM 12 Minutes

Night 5 of Night Weening

11:00PM 8 Minutes

4:00AM 8 Minutes

Night 6 Night Weening

11:00PM 5 Minutes

4:00AM None

Night 7 Night Weening

No feedings

There are many variations of night weaning for babies. Some parents of babies between five and nine months choose to keep one feeding each night for their baby. If you choose to keep one-night feeding, it's important to know that parents who choose to keep a night feeding often never achieve sleep success. If you absolutely must keep one-night feeding, be sure this feeding takes place around 11:00 PM, a few hours after your baby has gone to bed for the night. To wean the other feedings, follow the steps above but only for one of the night feedings. The other will remain in place but can be shortened in time if you choose. For nursing mothers who are worried about their milk supply, decreasing the offerings by minutes at a time will allow your body to adjust to the new normal. Once all night feedings are eliminated, you might choose to express your breast milk before going to bed each night to ensure that you keep up with your milk supply. Be patient with your body and do what feels right based on your needs and the needs of your baby. Everyone's supply is different.

Remain consistent throughout each night of the program and before you know it, you will be at night fourteen.

Chapter 9.
Conquering Naps

Now that you've mastered night sleep successfully, it's time to focus on naps. We have touched on naps in previous chapters, but we will dive in a bit deeper here. It is recommended that nap training does not occur until your baby is at least six months old. This is because its sleep-cycles are not where they need to be to fully train. Sleep cycles for babies typically last between thirty and forty minutes but each baby's cycle will vary. Before six months of age, babies wake up naturally after each sleep cycle and are unable to connect the cycles and put themselves back to sleep. If you take into consideration the time you spend rocking, nursing and snuggling your baby to sleep, by the time you put them down, if they have already fallen asleep, they will likely wake up confused and upset because you are no longer holding them. This can be incredibly upsetting for your baby and it will be very difficult for them to fall back to sleep after this. This is why it's recommended to encourage nap training once your baby has reached the six-month mark and not before this. If you start this process too soon, you're likely expecting something out of your baby that it is unable to developmentally achieve and process just yet. Even though you shouldn't begin to fully nap train until your baby is at the designated age, before this, you can work with your baby to help them begin the process of connecting their sleep cycles. This can be done first by identifying the length of your baby's sleep cycle. You will need to watch them closely on the monitor or in their room while it sleeps to see when it adjusts and moves between sleep cycles. Once you have been able to identify the length of time, you can quietly move into their room a few minutes before it transitions to the next sleep cycle and ultimately wakes up for a few minutes. When you're in their room, you can quietly soothe your baby by gently rubbing, tapping, or singing to your baby to soothe them into the next sleep cycle so that it doesn't fully wake up. Following these steps will help set your baby up for success when it's time to nap train. It will already be familiar with what it takes to move from one sleep cycle to the next and how to stay asleep throughout the process and the full duration of the nap.

Do not get consumed by the set nap times that you have in place. If a baby is tired, it can sleep outside of these times. Babies will change over time. There will be days they wake up more rested than others. Just like adults, there will be days when your baby wakes up tired and groggy. These days, it's helpful to pay extra attention to their sleepy cues and put them down for a nap when it shows you that it is tired. Parents often get consumed with the nap schedule and they choose to not let their baby nap when it is tired if this occurs outside of its normal nap time. This can impact naps for the rest of the day because if your baby shows you that it is tired and you choose to push through and not put them down to sleep, you might not be able to put them down when it's their actual naptime. When this happens, it's usually because your baby has moved beyond the initial tired and sleepy phase and now they have their second wind of energy. This second wind, just as we've mentioned before will give them an added boost of energy and they will be unable to sleep. They will be up and ready to keep playing. This could very well impact their night sleep as they might be overly tired at bedtime and unable to sleep. Parents often follow the common myth that if your baby doesn't nap during the day, it will be extra tired at night and this is simply not true. As a reminder, babies sleep much better at night if they have slept well throughout the day. That being said, you really want to try and find a good balance of encouraging a naptime routine and schedule while adjusting when your baby has different needs. You want to remain as consistent as possible while adapting to changing situations with your baby. For example, if you normally put your baby down for a nap two hours after it wakes up in the morning and then you start switching to four hours after it wakes up and then back to two hours, this will be very confusing for your baby. It won't understand when the best time is to nap and it will switch back and forth from being tired at different times of the day. Keeping your naps around the same time each day will significantly help give your baby the consistency that it needs. They will be able to predict when a nap is approaching and will then be able to prepare.

Naps will go over more smoothly if your baby is familiar with the space where it will be sleeping. Most naps should take place in a baby crib or bassinet. Parents often choose to allow their baby to sleep in a play yard and that's ok too. Just as long as the sleep location is clear of toys, blankets, bumpers, or anything else that could potentially be hazardous for a baby. You will want to think of naps just as you do night sleep to be sure the space is consistent and safe. Even though your baby will be sleeping during naps for much less time, it should be set up just like it would be for night sleep. For naps, you are in control of how dark you keep the room. Darkness is a sleep cue but if your child will be napping at daycare for example, where it won't be that dark, you might wish to train them to sleep in both environments. If all of this doesn't work for your baby and it still is not asleep after one hour, remove them from their crib, turn on a light and get them to do something active. You can try again after another hour has passed.

The ultimate goal of nap training is to introduce and develop sleep initiation with your baby. The main idea with sleep initiation is that we want your baby to ultimately be able to extend or initiate their nap when we provide the appropriate environment and naptime consistently overtime. We will be focused on sleep pressure with your baby. By identifying sleep times and following a consistent routine before each nap, we will ultimately be "pressuring" or encouraging your baby to sleep. When sleep pressure is high enough your baby gets to a place where it has no other choice but to fall asleep. It will know that the time has come, the environment is prepared and now all that's left is for them to take initiative and allow itself to nap. They will begin to get used to this routine and the actions that follow and eventually, they will begin following along with what is expected of them- sleep. The more it follows this routine, the more its body will adapt to napping at these specific times during the day. We want your baby to begin understanding that sleep and play happen at different times of the day. We want them to start associating changes in its environment and behaviors with what is coming next. When we work with our babies in this way, we are setting them up with a plan and routine that's easy for them to follow, and over time, they will begin to understand and prepare appropriately. Be patient with the process. The more consistent your routine and the more diligent you are with following the appropriate steps, the more likely you will be to find success with naps for your baby. In time, your baby will get better and more consistent with the new skill that it has learned. They will likely even look forward to his naps. This might take some time to develop but babies begin to understand that they feel better once they have had their nap and they feel as though they have recharged. With time and practice, your baby will be able to connect the two and will then look forward to the time of the day that allows them to rest and build up the energy that it needs to keep playing!

Naps are a critical part of your baby and future toddler's daily schedule. It's truly best to begin working on your baby at a point when it is waking up in the morning rested. This does not by any means, mean that nights need to be mastered at this point. It doesn't mean that your baby has stopped waking up at night altogether. It simply means that before you begin working on naps, you want to be sure that at this point, your baby is now waking up for short periods before putting themselves back to sleep. Even if it takes them some time to do so. To be clear, if your baby is still struggling with long periods of wakefulness at night, you find them constantly crying and waking up tired and irritable, now might not be the best time to nap train your baby. Naps are a critical component of your child's development and will also be vital to help ensure your baby gets a good night's sleep. Once your baby is ready to nap train, you can work to identify a good schedule for you both to follow. That being said, this is not something you want to take lightly. You do not want to put off nap training your baby as each nap and hour of sleep that your baby gets is vital. Your healthy infant will need lots of energy and fuel to get through their day of activities and the only way to get this type of energy is from healthy amounts of sleep each and every day. Frequent naps throughout the day will allow time to recharge and prepare for the next few hours of constant learning and development. Research shows that babies who sleep more throughout the day can learn more from their environment. This is because they can focus and concentrate much easier when they are fully rested. They are also able to maintain their attention for much longer periods. This information clearly shows the importance of naps and just how critical they are for your baby's development. While this information pertains to your baby and future toddler, research does not tell us at what point we should stop naps altogether. If it makes sense for you and your family, feel free to continue to include naps for your child as it continues to grow older.

We all need naps from time to time and children, as they grow will likely continue needing the added boost of sleep. That being said, just like night sleep, we can work to improve your baby's naps with several different strategies. These strategies are not one size fits all. You will need to work alongside your baby to determine the best strategy and plan for you and your family. But this guide will help you get started and it will also give you options. When working on your nap schedule and routine, you want to take into consideration a few things. Take a look at your parenting style, the behaviors that your baby exhibits, and other factors that might impact their sleep schedule throughout the day. You will also need to identify the amount of time you can truly dedicate to putting your baby down for a nap. Each family and parent might be different given their situation. Some parents work from home while others have multiple children to care for. All of these circumstances must be taken into consideration when coordinating your baby's nap schedule. Your baby will need quite a bit of sleep each day and this will be broken up into a few naps during the day and a long stretch of sleep at night. Depending on the age of your baby, it will need multiple naps during the day. For babies aged four to six months, they will need two to three naps spread out throughout the day. A general rule is to offer your baby a nap every two to two and a half hours. At this point, your baby has likely used enough energy and played enough that it's time for them to rest. We want to be sure that when we put our babies down for their nap that they are not overly tired. If we wait too long to put them down, they might get irritated, frustrated, and overly tired. At that point, they might even skip their nap because we waited too long and missed their sleep cues.

Sleep cues are ways that babies tell us they are tired and ready for sleep. If we know what to look out for, we will be able to identify the signs and get them ready for their nap as soon as it tells us that it is ready. Babies will show us when they're tired, hungry, hurt, or in need of a little extra tender loving care. We just have to be aware of what to look for. This takes some time and effort on our end and we must pay close attention to our baby and what they are telling us. This will come in time and the more you get to know your baby, the easier it will be to identify what it is it truly needs. Remember, these cues will change over time but to get started, we will cover a few of the common sleep cues that we see babies showing us. Common sleepy cues can be rubbing eyes, yawning, tugging at ears. Sleepy cues can also involve looking dazed and generally being less interested in the activities around. Once we identify the cues that our babies show us, we can act quickly when we see them and put them down for a nap. That being said, we must be paying attention! This is critical. We all get busy during the day and then suddenly, we realize too much time has passed and now it's too late to put them down for a nap. If we miss the point when our babies are tired, they will get a second wind and in turn, it will be incredibly difficult to get your baby to sleep. When babies get a second wind, they can let go of any tiredness they were initially feeling, and they now have a surge of energy. This energy encourages them to want to be up and active and avoid sleep. At this point, if a baby moves into this phase, it is more likely to fight its nap or skip it altogether. The second wind is a common reason why parents and caregivers struggle significantly when it comes to naps. We simply wait too long to put our baby down and move beyond the sleep sweet spot. The key here is to pay attention to your baby. Truly pay attention to the cues and actions your baby is consistently showing you. Don't be afraid to pay attention to the cues and try different things until you figure out what it is your child needs. When we pay close attention, put in time and effort, and prepare appropriately, we will find that this amount of work will lead our baby to sleep success. Along with paying attention to the cues it is showing us, we should also be mindful of the time. By paying attention to the time, you will know when to move your baby into its room to wind down for naptime.

Chapter 10.
Baby let's get some sleep!

Congratulations! You've made it through the two-week sleep training program. Now you should be enjoying much more restful nights and productive days. You probably can't believe that you and your baby are sleeping through the entire night with limited or no feedings at all. This is a huge accomplishment and you should be incredibly proud of yourself for pushing through when times were hard. You pushed through and persevered even when you felt like quitting. When your baby cried so much that your heart broke and when you felt like you should just hold your baby and let them sleep so they would stop crying. This was a tough and very necessary journey to go along but you did it. You followed all of the necessary steps and you made it through the program. Now you have a great sleeper who can soothe itself to sleep at night once you've followed its bedtime routine. You've accomplished your goal! You and your baby probably feel much better now that you're getting the rest you need. With all of that said, there are a few things that you will want to keep in mind as your baby continues to grow and move through developmental changes. At different points during your baby's time spent as an infant and toddler, you might find that different experiences could potentially lead to sleep disturbances. That being said, you might find the need to retrain your baby as time goes on and it's needed. For example, if it hasn't started already, your child will begin teething. The teething process can begin very early for some babies, at just a few months old and for others, it might take quite a bit of time before they see a tooth appear. Regardless of what the teething timeframe looks like for your baby, teething can be incredibly difficult for babies as they are experiencing pain that can't be controlled.

Don't assume that your baby will experience teething symptoms, but you want to be prepared and know the signs to look out for if it does experience pain and other symptoms. The pain felt from teething has been known to cause a variety of symptoms and can also lead to sleep issues. Babies might begin to drool excessively, and they will also want to chew on everything. Other signs and symptoms of teething include diarrhea caused by excess saliva that can make your baby's bowel movement runnier than normal circumstances. Excess drool can also cause rashes around your baby's mouth that are irritating. You might even find that your baby begins to rub or pull its ears while it's teething. It's important to identify the clear signs of teething that way you will know how to address this issue if you find that teething is interrupting their sleep. Some babies might get upset and cranky when a tooth is just about ready to pop through while others keep playing and don't exhibit any symptoms. Babies might experience multiple night waking, want to nurse excessively for comfort and others will sleep right through the teething process. If you are nursing and find that they are nursing excessively, be sure to set limits on how much you let your baby nurse at a time. Many babies often revert back to unhealthy sleep habits because they end up relying on nursing as a crutch to give them comfort while they're nursing, and they also use nursing to help fall asleep because of the amount of pain they might be in. It will be difficult to set a limit with your nursing times during teething, but you must do so to ensure it doesn't completely revert back to relying on this sleep crutch.

As a parent, you will want to be prepared for all case scenarios. Researchers have been known to say that teething does not interfere with a baby's sleep but most parents who have gone through this experience with their children will completely disagree. If your baby is experiencing pain while teething and it's interfering with their sleep, you will want to be sure it is as comfortable as possible to encourage sleep. More likely than not, if you find that your baby is now waking up multiple times throughout the night when they were previously sleeping peacefully, teething pain is at the root. During this time, you might want to try a cold washcloth that you or your baby can hold on their gums. Babies often find the cooling sensation very soothing and this could ease their pain a bit before bed. If they are extra fussy, a pediatrician approved over-the-counter medication like acetaminophen or ibuprofen can be used and has been known to be incredibly helpful. Addressing pain right as it's approaching will work best for your baby. You will want to give this medication to your baby about forty-five minutes before bedtime for it to be most effective. This will help to ensure they are comfortable by the time they're ready to fall asleep. Parents have often reported that when they gave this type of medication to their child while teething, they were once again able to sleep throughout the night. Before giving your child any medication, you must discuss this with your pediatrician. They will be able to recommend the best over-the-counter medication and will also prescribe the proper dosage. You will also want to avoid giving medication to your baby every night. We do not want them to rely on this to get them through but rather to utilize medication as a tool when necessary. Some alternatives have been known to significantly help babies sleep when they are teething. Holistic remedies have become increasingly popular and easy to use. Many parents choose to massage different types of essential oils and natural herbs on their baby's gums. Do your research ahead of time if you choose this option to treat teething pain and irritation. If you choose to use a natural alternative, be sure that this too has been approved by your doctor. When in doubt, ask and find out. The last thing you want to happen is to try something new without your doctor's approval and you end up needing to call because your baby had a negative reaction. Always be sure to stay ahead of this by confirming with your doctor and making sure everything given to your baby has been cleared. Clearing everything with your doctor doesn't guarantee that your baby will respond negatively to something, but it helps avoid at least some potential obstacles and negative reactions that could be experienced by your baby. Keep in mind that teething will last around two years, so you want to find a consistent method now to ensure you stick to your sleep routine as much as possible.

Other factors that might impact your baby's sleep are travel and illness. When you travel with your baby, it might be thrown off by time changes, impacted daily routine and it might be overwhelmed with all the new experiences it just had. Traveling with your baby can be fun and challenging. Before you travel, you will want to start with a well-rested baby. Do everything you possibly can to ensure that your baby is rested and has slept well in the days before your trip. An overtired baby almost guarantees a frustrating and stressful vacation. Traveling with your baby can also wreak havoc on the well-established sleep routine that you have set in place. If you fly or travel by car, your baby will not only be outside of its comfort zone, but will also be unable to sleep in its crib and its room like it normally would. Your baby will now need to adjust to a new environment and learn how to balance new experiences while getting the sleep it needs. While you travel, it's important to stick to your baby's normal routine as much as possible. This might be easier said than done but if at the very least, you can try to keep your baby's nap time around the same time, it will be helpful for you once you return home. Traveling in general can impact adult sleep and baby sleep due to all the changes that come along with travel. You will also want to plan your travel around accommodations for your baby. If you're staying in a hotel, try booking a room with a living room or an extra bedroom. This will allow your baby to have its own space to nap in and rest for the night. If the room is too small, the likelihood of getting your baby to sleep at the designated time while still enjoying your vacation is slim. If there is an extra room available, you can leave your baby to sleep at its normal bedtime and still enjoy the space in another room. This could make for an expensive vacation, but it will be worth it if your baby can get the rest it needs even when away from home. Try to get one good nap in each day if you're traveling. This will help your baby to get the restorative sleep that it needs. If possible, this nap should take place in a crib, play yard or bassinet rather than on the go. Babies sleep much better in a baby bed rather than in a car or stroller. You can try squeezing in the nap earlier in the day so that you will have the rest of the day to enjoy and explore. Your baby will likely take another nap on the go and that's ok. It will need it! The goal here is to ensure at least one of its daily naps is restorative and deep. This will help them sleep much better at night and will ensure that it is recharging and gaining more energy to get them through the rest of the day.

Trying to be as prepared as possible before you travel will help you stay on track as much as possible. For example, when you travel with your baby, be sure to take along all the sleep supplies you will need. This does not mean that you will be able to take everything, like the crib for example, but take as many items as you can and that makes sense to bring along. A few items that make sense to bring along include a sleep sack or wearable blanket for your baby, a lovey if your baby has one, a portable sound machine, a portable baby monitor a portable crib if you have one for your baby. Remember, these are items that your baby is familiar with. They bring them peace and comfort and allow them to sleep well throughout the night. If you can, do whatever you can to bring as many items as possible without feeling like you're over packed for your vacation. If you're bringing a portable crib, they can often be folded down and are much smaller in size than regular cribs which make them easy to travel with. If you don't have a travel crib and you're staying at a hotel, be sure to call ahead to see if the hotel you're staying at has a travel crib they can bring into your room. If you're staying with friends or family, ask ahead of time if they have a spare room where your baby can sleep. If this is not possible, do whatever you can to create a barrier in the room that you are sharing with your baby. This should be a safe barrier of some kind that will allow your baby to have its own small space in the room that you are staying in.

You want to be sure that we mimic your baby's sleep environment as close as possible. Making sure your baby sleeps in a crib is not only the safest option for your baby but it will also give your baby the consistency that it needs considering it is now familiar with sleeping in its own space. Often times, parents skip this step and think their baby will sleep just fine in the bed with them. Co-sleeping is for some families but it's not for all as it can potentially be very dangerous. To ensure that your child is safe and sleeps well, make arrangements to have a crib available. If you assume that they will sleep in bed with you and it rejects this idea, this can turn into an incredibly difficult and frustrating situation quickly. Staying prepared ahead of time will help ease the transition into your normal routine once you return home.

Illness can also impact the work that you've done in sleep training your baby. When a baby is sick and needs extra comfort, this is not the time to leave them alone in their crib. They will likely need to nurse or bottle-feed more often to get the extra comfort and nutrients that it needs. If you're like most parents, it will be difficult to leave your baby alone while they are sick and not feeling well and that's normal. This is a time to ensure your baby gets well and then you can resume sleep training once the time is right and your baby is feeling better. Illness can throw off your baby's routine and sleep schedule significantly. The goal here is to get your baby well and feeling better and then you can try getting back on track. As your baby continues to grow and develop there will likely be a variety of occurrences that interfere with their sleep. Even something as simple as overstimulation can greatly impact your baby because it has so much to think about. It's important to keep all of this in mind as you move through each stage with your baby.

We've now covered a few potential obstacles that might interfere with your baby's sleep schedule and routine. This is not a full list of all that can throw your baby off of their sleep schedule but they are meant to give you an idea of what to be on the lookout for and how you can prepare as much as possible before these obstacles come into play. Remember that even if your baby is sleeping great now, this can change in the future and you will have to retrain your baby. No matter how many times of the coming months and years that you must retrain your baby, you must remain consistent with the program. You might need to alter the program as time goes on due to changes with your baby but remembering to stay consistent will lead you to successful sleep. Remember to always pay close attention to the needs of your baby as it moves through different physical and emotional developmental stages. These stages will call for different needs and adjustments to ensure it gets the sleep that it needs at different stages of its life. It's our job as parents to always pay close attention to what our babies need. Sleep training is not a one size fits all program. Each baby is different and will have different needs now and in time that must be customized. Do not let the difficulties of this program prevent you from following through with it in the future if needed. Remember that you are a great parent and you're doing everything you can to give your baby what it needs. Be mindful to not compare yourself to other parents who say their babies are sleeping or overcoming other obstacles. Your baby was chosen for you and you are the best parent for your baby. Do not let comparisons and other negative thoughts impact how you parent or the choices you make for your baby. Stay focused on your baby and their needs and you will find success no matter what life throws at you. Always remember to keep the goal in mind and give your baby the tools it needs to be a good sleeper. Go back to your journal, look through the notes that you've taken throughout this process, and constantly remind yourself of the importance of sleep training your baby. Don't let societal pressures, busy schedules, or other obstacles interfere with what your baby needs. Stay focused on your parenting style and do not let others impact what you choose to do and how you choose to handle sleep training with your baby. You, as their parent knows better than anyone else what they need. You will make the best decisions for your baby regardless of what others around you might want you to do. Sleep training will take a great deal of time and patience on your end but with a positive attitude, confidence, consistency, and the end goal in mind, you will be able to persevere and help your baby along its journey no matter the pit stops that you might fall into. Know that there are a variety of resources available for you and your family, stay positive, and keep climbing!

Happy sleeping!